DEFENDING
the ACCUSED

DEFENDING
the ACCUSED

Stories from the Courtroom

by Richard Wormser

Franklin Watts
A Division of Scholastic Inc.
New York • Toronto • London • Aucklund • Sydney
Mexico City • New Delhi • Hong Kong
Danbury, Connecticut

To Ruth and Bill Lubic:
For their friendship and hospitality

Interior design by Molly Heron
Photographs ©: Archive Photos: 39 (Reuters), 44 (Reuters/Pool); Arkansas Democrat Gazette: 83, 86, 93; Arkansas Department of Correction: 80, 89, 95; Corbis-Bettmann: 41, 49, 50, 56 (Reuters); Dale Yates: 97; Lifecodes Corporation: 42 top (Dianne Baasch Maio), 42 bottom; Lynne Stewart: 51, 59; New York City Police Department: 20; Richard Wormser: 9, 17, 21, 23, 65, 66, 68, 71; The State Newspaper, Columbia SC: 109, 114.

.

Visit Franklin Watts on the Internet at:
http://publishing.grolier.com

Library of Congress Cataloging-in-Publication Data

Wormser, Richard, 1933–
      Defending the accused : stories from the courtroom / Richard Wormser.
          p. cm.
      Includes bibliographical references and index.
      Summary: Presents case histories that illustrate the role of and techniques
          used by defense lawyers in the American judicial system.
      ISBN 0-531-11378-7
      1. Public defenders—United States—Juvenile literature. 2. Defense (Criminal
procedure)—United States—Juvenile literature. [1. Defense (Criminal procedure)
2. Public defenders. 3. Justice, Administration of 4. Lawyers.] I. Title.

KF9646.Z9 W67 2001
345.73'01—dc21   00-033036

Contents

"How Can You Defend Those People?"

It was March 5, 1770. The mob was furious and the eight soldiers were terrified. Britain had imposed new taxes on the American colonies and the people of Boston were outraged. They poured into the streets to protest. British soldiers were called to the scene. They were forced to defend themselves against the unruly mob. Five people were killed. The killings, known as the Boston Massacre, inflamed the city. Throughout the thirteen colonies, the people demanded that the soldiers—whether or not they had actually fired on the crowd—be punished and that some of them be hanged.

Their defense lawyer was John Adams of Boston, Massachusetts, soon to become one of the great leaders of the American Revolution (1775–1783).

Adams was angered by the killings. He was also upset by Britain's stubborn refusal to grant the colonies greater freedom. But he felt that anger must give way to law. Because there was a danger that innocent people might suffer for the crimes of the guilty, Adams eloquently argued:

> *[It is] more beneficial that many guilty persons should escape unpunished than one innocent person should suffer. The reason is because it is of more importance to the community that innocence should be protected than it is that guilt should be punished.*

Adam's argument prevailed. Only two soldiers were lightly punished. The rest were discharged from the accusation, or acquitted.

Although Adams tried the case under British law, the principle of protecting the innocent has been a major pillar of the American criminal justice system. The law states that (1) a defendant must be considered innocent until proven guilty, (2) a defendant is entitled to a fair and speedy trial, (3) a defendant cannot be forced or threatened into testifying against himself, and (4) a defendant should be found innocent or guilty based only on the evidence presented in court.

In fact, violations of these principles sometimes occur. Police officers may coerce confessions. Prosecutors may withhold evidence that favors the accused to get a conviction. Witnesses sometimes make mistakes or give false testimony. Judges or juries may be prejudiced against defendants.

The justice system angers defense attorney Steve

Pokart. "I see injustice all the time," he explains. "If the society we live in were really just and fair, unprejudiced and humane, most of my clients wouldn't have grown up to be my clients in the first place. The people I deal with are desperate, they're angry, they're afraid,

Defense attorney Steve Pokart (right) speaks with a client outside a criminal court building in New York City.

and they're really hurting. Justice abandoned them before they got to me."

The only way most people accused of a crime can protect themselves in court is to have a competent defense attorney. Defense lawyers are essential to the American legal system because most trials are based on the principle of advocacy. That means that lawyers representing each side—the defense and prosecution—try to prove the innocence or guilt of the accused in front of a judge or jury.

The odds usually favor the prosecution because its lawyers often have more money and resources to convict a defendant than a defense attorney has to build the defendant's case. Of course, wealthy defendants can afford first-rate lawyers, investigators to dig up evidence in their favor, and specialists to testify on their behalf. Impoverished defendants do not have those options. Their best hope is to find a dedicated and experienced lawyer willing to represent them. This is not easy. Lawyers available to poor defendants may be ignorant of the law, have poor courtroom skills, or be unmotivated. Some have even fallen asleep during the trial!

State public defender organizations and private agencies such as the Legal Aid Society provide lawyers for those who cannot afford them in criminal, civil, and juvenile cases. The courts also assign cases to lawyers in private practice for reduced fees as part of their public service. Some defense lawyers who feel strongly about particular cases work without pay, or pro bono, which means "for the good" in Latin. Many excellent lawyers represent poor people despite the low pay because they are committed to justice and believe that all defendants have a right to competent legal representation in the courtroom.

Defense lawyers can represent clients in civil and criminal cases. Civil law governs rights and regulations in business, personal injury, and governmental matters. Suits against tobacco or pharmaceutical companies for damages are examples of civil cases. However, this book examines criminal defense lawyers who take on unpopular cases.

In this book, we will see defense lawyers working on a cross section of cases. The cases described in the first three chapters focus on the trial level. We will see how defense lawyers challenge eyewitness testimony, attempt to refute, or prove wrong, scientific evidence, and try to neutralize ethnic prejudice in the courtroom. The case described in the fourth chapter shows how a defense lawyer handles a criminal case involving a ten-year-old child. The cases in the last two chapters deal with the appeals process—the legal proceedings required to overturn a guilty verdict.

Since people who enter the criminal court system are often guilty of some crime, people may ask: Why would a defense attorney represent a guilty person? Former criminal defense lawyer James Kunen writes that when he was working in the criminal courts in Washington, D.C., he was frequently asked, "How can you defend those people?" He replied as follows: "Because the question presumes that 'those people' accused of crimes are guilty and that people who are guilty of crimes ought not to be defended, it reflects a profound misunderstanding of our criminal justice system and the defense attorney's role in it."

If accused of a crime, everyone in society, no matter

what the charge, is entitled to a defense attorney. And that defense attorney is required to defend the client, guilty or innocent, as well as he or she possibly can.

"Many of us have our ideals," Pokart cautions. "But we also know that our clients don't want ideals, they want results. They want to stay out of jail or get out of jail. And that's what our job is."

 # Murder at the Red Door

PROSECUTOR:	What did you hear?
WITNESS:	A gunshot.
PROSECUTOR:	What did you see?
WITNESS:	Danny fall to the floor.
PROSECUTOR:	Can you describe to the jury how he fell?
WITNESS:	He fell slowly and on his back.

In the case described in this chapter, defense attorney Steve Pokart represented a man charged with murder who was unable to pay for a lawyer. Pokart had to convince the jury that there was a reasonable doubt that his client committed the murder, despite the fact that there were eyewitnesses. Reasonable doubt *is a basic principle of law. It means that if a jury believes there is a reasonable doubt that a person committed a crime, then it must find the defendant not guilty.*

"If you go to trial," Steve Pokart explained to Nathaniel Wright, "you may get twenty-five, thirty, forty years to life. If you plead guilty, the district attorney has offered you twelve years minus time for good behavior. That's not a bad deal."

Nathaniel (Nat) Wright was arrested for shooting sixteen-year-old Danny Hernandez in a crowded social club in New York City. Pokart, a public defender from the Legal Aid Society, was assigned to defend Wright in court.

The criminal division of Legal Aid gets its funding from New York City. When someone charged with a crime is first brought to court, he is assigned an attorney, usually from Legal Aid, if he cannot afford one. Legal Aid lawyers do not handle many murder trials. Most of their cases involve robbery, larceny, minor assaults, domestic violence, or nuisance crimes such as sneaking into the subway, sleeping on a park bench, or riding a bicycle without a bell. In this case, Nat Wright's file was put in a basket with a number of other cases and Steve Pokart picked it up.

Pokart explained his client's options to him. Wright listened but showed little response. He was calm, his eyes expressionless and his face blank. Pokart later said that Wright was one of the coolest characters he had ever met. He never saw Wright smile or show concern.

"No," Wright finally replied in a low, steady voice. "I'd rather go to trial."

Pokart nodded. "It's your call," he said. "But I warn you that the district attorney says he has three witnesses who claim they saw you shoot and kill Danny Hernandez. If we go to trial, you'll see what a good trial lawyer I am—and you'll probably lose the case."

"Somehow, I don't think they'll testify," Wright answered in a flat voice.

The question of Wright's guilt or innocence was not for Pokart to decide. His job as a public defender is to defend his clients. He explains:

If my client wants to go to trial and claim he is innocent, and there are a hundred witnesses who say they saw him do it, my job is to carry out his wishes and go to trial. If he wants to plead guilty, then my job is to help him get as light a sentence as possible. My clients may lie about their innocence, but those whose job it is to uphold the law also lie. Police sometimes lie when they testify in court. Prosecutors sometimes lie. Some judges ignore the law. And even jurors lie.

Most people accused of crimes do not go to trial. They know if they are convicted in court, they will receive a much harsher sentence than if they accept a plea bargain. A plea bargain is an agreement between the defendant, the prosecution, and the judge in which the defendant agrees to plead guilty to a lesser charge. While judges must accept the guilty plea, they are not legally bound by the prosecutor's recommendations about the sentence. Some federal judges impose harsher sentences if they feel that the plea bargain is too lenient.

Most public defenders welcome the chance to defend their client in court. Pokart, who once dreamed of a career in the theater, loves to fight for a client in the courtroom. A good courtroom lawyer needs to be a good performer. Pokart enjoys the emotional rush of testing his skills and knowledge of the law against a tough prosecutor trying to convict his client.

However, it makes sense to go to trial only if there is a chance of winning. In the case of *People of the State of New York v. Nathaniel Wright*, Pokart had mixed feelings. "If the district attorney is right," he said, "and he has three eyewitnesses who saw my client kill someone, we have a real uphill battle to fight."

The charge against Wright was murder in the second degree. That means there was no intent to kill or the killing was impulsive. Wright had three previous arrests, two of them involving criminal possession of narcotics. The third was an assault charge. He threw a glass bottle at his girlfriend's face. She required twenty stitches.

The prosecution believed Wright wanted to go to trial because he knew the witnesses were too frightened to testify against him. The witnesses might have been worried that Wright, who lived in their neighborhood, would hurt or even kill them for testifying.

Months before the trial, Pokart and his associate, Rebecca Rosenfeld, began to prepare their case. They started by determining how strong the evidence against Nat Wright was.

Like Steve Pokart, Rebecca Rosenfeld is a tough idealist. She feels that the system is stacked against the poor. While many of her clients are guilty of crimes, she feels that society's crimes against them are even greater. When people ask her how she can represent guilty people, Rosenfeld replies, "If you want to represent innocent people, you shouldn't be doing this line of work. Whether guilty or innocent, my clients have a right to an attorney—just like rich people."

It also bothers Rosenfeld that people assume that because she is a public defender, she couldn't succeed

Defense attorneys Steve Pokart and Rebecca Rosenfeld believe strongly that anyone accused of a crime has the right to an attorney, whether or not he or she is guilty.

as a corporate lawyer. Rosenfeld explains, "We could all have gotten high-paying jobs after law school. Many of my classmates went into corporate law on Wall Street starting at $90,000 a year. But I didn't want to spend my life reshuffling rich people's money around. My job involves me with people I care for and respect. Many of my clients are victimizers but they are also victims of an unjust social system."

Before the trial began, Rosenfeld and two Legal Aid investigators made several visits to the families and friends of Wright and Hernandez. It didn't help much, according to Rosenfeld:

Usually you can find something in an investigation that will help your client. I was not able to find anything. It was very frustrating. People would shut the door in my face when I went to call on them. Or they made appointments and failed to show up. One woman denied she saw anything and later on appeared in court and admitted that she saw the shooting but not the face of the killer. Another person was supposed to have valuable information, but all I got out of him was mumbo-jumbo.

Rosenfeld discovered that the victim was involved in drug dealing and sold crack cocaine. Later she heard rumors that Hernandez had insulted Wright's sister. But no one, including defendant Nat Wright, was willing to reveal any solid information.

More than a year after the murder, the trial began. The judge was the grandfatherly Nicholas Figueroa. Unlike some judges, he listens patiently when the defense challenges him.

The first task was to choose a jury of twelve men and women and four alternates. Every day, Wright was brought to the courtroom in handcuffs, which were removed before the prospective jurors entered. On his first day in court, Wright wore a white jacket adorned with a LUGZ Jeans advertisement. He listened closely to the proceedings without saying anything. From time to time, Rosenfeld discussed the selection of jurors with him.

Pokart and Rosenfeld analyzed the pros and cons of each prospective juror. Both sides have the right to challenge twenty jurors. They tried to eliminate jurors who might be hostile to their client.

"We tried to eliminate potential jurors with teenage sons or who were involved with teenagers because we feared that they might react negatively to our client [since] the deceased was only sixteen. We wanted a jury that would be fair and impartial," said Rosenfeld.

Pokart decided not to put his client on the witness stand. It is a defendant's right to sit silently during the entire trial. By law, the defense is not required to prove anything. The burden of proof lies with the prosecution. The prosecution must prove beyond a reasonable doubt that the accused person committed the crime.

After three days, the jury was selected. It was time for the trial to start. The trial began with opening arguments to the jury.

Representing the prosecution, Ray Marinaccio described the crime in his opening argument. He charged that on the morning of October 12, 1996, at 2:30 A.M., Nathaniel Wright was at a social club called the Red Door when he shot and killed Danny Hernandez.

"The bullet entered his stomach . . . ripped through his intestines and exited out his back," said Marinaccio.

Marinaccio then described how Hernandez's friend, Joseph Santoro, pulled out his gun and began firing at Wright. The two men shot at each other for several seconds in the crowded club. People screamed and dropped to the floor or tried to reach the exits. By the time the firing stopped, eight people had been wounded. Wright and Santoro were not injured. Marinaccio claimed that Wright was the killer and that the prosecution would prove this beyond a reasonable doubt.

A police photograph of the social club in which Danny Hernandez was shot and killed

Steve Pokart rose to make his opening argument. Like most good lawyers, he feels that his first and last statements to a jury are crucial. He works immediately to plant the seeds of doubt in the minds of the jury. He told the jurors to note whether a single witness says, "I saw Nathan Wright take a gun out, approach Mr. Hernandez with a gun in his hands, aim the gun and pull the trigger, heard a bang, and saw Danny Hernandez go down." Pokart also pointed out that there was no evidence to link his client to the killing.

"You will find that the case against Nathaniel Wright has not been proven beyond a reasonable doubt . . . and you will let one innocent man go home," Pokart concluded.

Then it was time for the witness testimony. Christina Flores, a friend of Danny Hernandez, was called to the stand. She said she was dancing with Angel (Danny's street name) when she heard a shot fired. She turned and saw Danny on the floor. She said she did not see the gunman.

Several police officers then provided testimony about their investigation of the crime scene. While their testimony did not link Wright to the murder, Pokart cross-examined them in order to point out errors they might have made. One police officer admitted he had made a mistake about the number of bullets he found. Another stated that he did not carefully examine the lighting in the club at the time of the

Steve Pokart addresses the jury during his opening statements.

shooting. A third said he did not ask a witness how much he had been drinking and whether he was using drugs at the time of the shoot-out. By suggesting that the police did sloppy work, Pokart hoped that the jury might doubt that the prosecution could prove Wright committed the crime.

Throughout the trial, Pokart fiercely defended his client's interests. He raised numerous objections when the prosecutor asked the witnesses questions that Pokart believed might prejudice the jury against his client. And he risked antagonizing the judge by challenging the judge's rulings.

For example, Pokart clashed with the judge over a reenactment of the location of the victim when he was shot. During the testimony of one witness, the prosecutor asked the witness to tell him where to stand to show what her position was in relation to Danny when he was shot. When Pokart asked the witness to do the same for him, he noticed that she placed him in a different position from the prosecutor. Pokart complained.

POKART:	The record should note . . . that that's not the position [where] Mr. Marinaccio was standing.
JUDGE FIGUEROA:	That's not for you to say. That's for the jury.
POKART:	It's for me to say. A record has to be made.
JUDGE FIGUEROA:	If you continue in this fashion, it will grow unpleasant. . . .

Judge Figueroa called Pokart to the bench where they talked out of the jury's hearing. "You cannot testify in front of this jury as to any difference between your demonstration and the prosecution. . . . I don't want any arguments in front of the jury. It's not going to become a circus," he told Pokart.

"I'm not trying to make it a circus. I'm trying to provide accurate information," replied Pokart. "You started in an argumentative fashion in front of this jury and I cannot allow that," Judge Figueroa said.

At times, Pokart asked the court not to allow certain testimony, such as that of the victim's mother. Other times, he complained to the judge about his sympathy for the prosecution. He didn't like the judge questioning the prosecution's witnesses.

Out of the jury's hearing, Steve Pokart and Rebecca Rosenfeld discuss a point of law with Judge Nicholas Figueroa.

"I think that's improper . . . and lends the authority of the court to Mr. Marinaccio's case," Pokart said. Surprisingly, Judge Figueroa agreed and promised to restrain himself. He later told Pokart that his objections were right.

"Then why do you overrule them?" Pokart asked. "Because you push the envelope," Judge Figueroa replied. Later, Pokart admitted that he does push the envelope, saying "It's my job to do so—as long as I don't make the judge hostile to my client and antagonize the jury."

On the fourth day of the trial, Antonia Reed, who saw the shooting, testified she saw a confrontation between Danny Hernandez and a stranger. She said:

I saw Danny standing by the bar. There was someone standing in front of him. His back was towards me and I didn't see his face. Suddenly Danny's face got real serious. I saw the man, he had a gun, he had a gun in his right hand and he pointed it towards Danny's lower body. There was a shot and suddenly Danny fell slowly and was on his back. As Danny fell to the ground, the male stood over him. Then I saw Joseph [Santoro] with a gun in his hand. I said to my friend, "Let's get out of here." As soon as we turned around to the back, the shooting began.

Reed maintained that she did not see the face of the shooter. Pokart believed she did. Based on the angle of the bullet, it was clear that Danny Hernandez's killer could not have been standing with his back to Reed. He had to be standing at least in profile. Pokart wanted to emphasize the idea that Reed recognized the gunman and did not identify him as Nat Wright. However, even though she admitted that she saw part of his face and could tell his shirt had no buttons in front, she steadfastly denied that she could identify the gunman.

The prosecution was having difficulty getting the two key witnesses to testify. Although they told the police and the grand jury that Wright was the killer, they refused to say so in court. Judge Figueroa issued a bench warrant for one witness, Archie Samuels. He was arrested at work and brought to court.

Archie Samuels was a reluctant witness. He was a big man, more than 6 feet (180 cm) tall. He was extremely uncomfortable on the stand, refusing to look at Wright. The prosecutor quickly established that he was a hostile witness and was brought to court involuntarily by the police. Samuels admitted that he had been a friend of Wright's for a number of years. They hung out together on the streets. He said Wright's street name was Lord. Samuels also admitted to a life of crime.

"I smoked crack, robbed people, stole. I did everything I could to earn money. Who didn't do those things?" he said.

On the night of the shooting, he was a bouncer at the Red Door. When the shooting began, he was checking people for weapons at the door as they entered. Suddenly a few patrons ran out of the club.

"I thought there was a fight going on so I rushed inside. I heard 'pop' 'pop' 'pop,' the sound of gunfire," he said.

Samuels said that he could see only one of the shooters, a person later identified as Joseph Santoro.

He said he did not recognize the other gunman. Prosecutor Marinaccio pressed him to admit that he told the police he saw Nathaniel Wright with a gun in his hand, but he denied it.

PROSECUTOR: When you looked out on the dance floor, did you see Nat Wright?

SAMUELS: Yes. I saw Nat Wright was pointing a gun at a Hispanic person.

PROSECUTOR: And what happened to the Hispanic man that pulled out the gun, what did he do?

SAMUELS: They were shooting at each other, returning fire.

PROSECUTOR: Did you tell Detective Rafferty "I saw Nat shooting Danny"?

SAMUELS: No.

PROSECUTOR: Did you tell Detective Rafferty "I saw sparks coming from Nat's gun and then the Spanish guy next to Danny started shooting at Nat"?

SAMUELS: No.

Samuels was finally forced to admit that he did tell the police and the grand jury that he saw Wright with a gun. He then said that the police pressured him and that he lied to the grand jury when he told them he saw Wright firing a gun.

Judge Figueroa then informed the jury that they could not consider Samuels's previous testimony to the police or grand jury as evidence of Wright's guilt. They could only use it to determine how credible Samuels was as a witness. Samuels insisted that the police pressured him into identifying Wright as the gunman. The prosecutor pushed Samuels to admit he saw Wright with a gun.

PROSECUTOR: Tell the jury who was firing that gun. Look at the jury, sir, and testify, sir.

SAMUELS: I seen Nat.

PROSECUTOR: What did you see him do?

SAMUELS: Fire a shot at somebody that was firing at him.

Later Archie Samuels admitted, "I saw sparks firing from Nat's gun and then the Spanish guy next to Danny starts firing at Nat."

Now it was Pokart's turn to cross-examine the witness. He seized on Samuels's denial that he knew who the shooter was. He also pointed out that Samuels had drunk a large amount of liquor, smoked a number of "blunts" (cigars filled with marijuana), and saw the shoot-out in a room with little light. Much more comfortable with the defense attorney, Samuels repeated his charge that the police pressured him to identify Nat Wright as the gunman. (Later, the police officer emphatically denied he coerced anyone.)

Pokart then tried to score another point with the jury by revealing that the prosecution discouraged Samuels from speaking with the defense before the trial.

POKART: We haven't met before, Mr. Samuels?

SAMUELS: No, but when I asked to speak with you, they told me it would be bad for me to speak with you.

POKART: Who did you ask?

SAMUELS: Mr. Marinaccio.

Pokart let this sink into the jury before continuing to question the witness.

POKART: You don't want to say something that is not true, do you?

SAMUELS: No.

POKART: You were sworn with an oath here, right?

SAMUELS: Yes.

POKART: You don't want to lie in front of the judge, do you?

SAMUELS: No.

POKART: You don't want to lie in front of this jury, right?

SAMUELS: Yes.

POKART: Mr. Marinaccio asked you a couple of times as to what you recognized in the club and once or twice you said well, yes, after a while I could see it was Nat shooting back at Santoro, but the police told you that later.

SAMUELS: Yes. Correct.

POKART: You knew it was not from observation because the cops told you that?

SAMUELS: Right.

POKART: You didn't want to fight with the cops.

SAMUELS: Right.

Pokart turned the witness over to the prosecution. Marinaccio now tried to show that Samuels had just lied.

PROSECUTOR: Isn't it a fact that you told the detective it was Nathaniel Wright who did the shooting before you looked at him inside the cell?

SAMUELS: No! No!

PROSECUTOR: Isn't it a fact that the detective wrote out the entire statement and you signed it before you looked at him in the cell?

SAMUELS: No!

PROSECUTOR: And isn't it a fact that you just looked at me a few moments ago and mouthed the word "sorry"?

SAMUELS: No.

PROSECUTOR: Sir. Are you lying?

SAMUELS: No.

The prosecutor planted in the jury's mind that Samuels was apologizing for reneging on his promise to testify by saying "sorry." It was a strong point and Pokart rose to rebut it.

POKART: Mr. Marinaccio asked you whether you mouthed the word "sorry." Mr. Samuels, you're sorry you're here today, aren't you?

SAMUELS: Yes.

POKART: You're sorry your ex-pal Mr. Wright is in jail.

SAMUELS: Yes. I am.

POKART: You're sorry he's accused of murder.

SAMUELS: Yes.

POKART: And you're sorry that a sixteen-year-old boy is dead.

SAMUELS: Yes.

POKART: You're sorry that eight people got shot.

SAMUELS: Yes.

POKART: So there are a lot of things you're sorry about.

The examination of Archie Samuels was over. Steve Pokart and Rebecca Rosenfeld felt that Samuels was not a good witness for the prosecution and they had a chance of winning the case.

The last witness was Danny Hernandez's close friend, Joseph Santoro. Immediately after the killing, he exchanged gunfire with the man who shot Hernandez. Because eight people were wounded in the shoot-out, Santoro was charged with reckless endangerment. In return for agreeing to testify against Wright, the state promised to reduce the charges against Santoro. In this agreement, Santoro would get a sentence of only two to four years instead of ten to twenty years. Santoro agreed to the deal and then changed his mind. So the judge sentenced him to eleven to twenty-two years in prison. Pokart believed, as long as Santoro refused to testify, there was no solid evidence against his client.

After Archie Samuels's appearance in court, Pokart got bad news. Joseph Santoro had agreed to testify if the prosecution asked the judge who sentenced him to reduce his term to two to four years. The prosecution agreed but warned Santoro it could not guarantee a reduced sentence. However, the sentence was likely to be reduced if Santoro cooperated.

Although Santoro was an acknowledged drug dealer, he looked more like an insecure teenager than a dangerous gunman. Uncomfortable on the stand, Santoro admitted that he agreed to testify in the hope that his sentence would be reduced. He also admitted that he led a life of crime before his conviction. He robbed and he sold drugs, mostly crack cocaine.

On the day of the murder, he and Danny Hernandez spent the day together celebrating

Santoro's eighteenth birthday. Santoro admitted he drank a half bottle of champagne, some vodka, and some beer, and smoked a small amount of marijuana. He also admitted to carrying a 9-millimeter pistol that Hernandez had given him.

SANTORO: As we [Santoro and Hernandez] was talking, this individual here was looking in my face with the type of face like something was going to happen that night, violence or whatever was the case.

PROSECUTOR: Can you look around the courtroom and tell me if you see the individual that was looking at you?

SANTORO: Yes. He's right there.

Santoro pointed to Nat Wright. Santoro says he went to get some people he knew to let them know that "something might go down right there." Suddenly he heard a noise that at first he thought was "a bottle dropping."

SANTORO: I turned around and I seen Danny fall to the floor. I saw the individual who shot Danny. Mr. Nathaniel Wright pointed a gun towards my way. So I pulled my gun out. I tried to shoot him as well.

According to Santoro, the two men fired at each other while people ran for safety, screaming and shouting. Santoro then testified that he identified Wright in the police lineup several days later.

Pokart then cross-examined Santoro. He tried to portray him as an unreliable drug dealer whose testimony could not be trusted. Pokart asked him why he reneged on his original agreement to testify. Santoro maintained that he was young and didn't know what he was doing.

POKART: You were old enough to carry a 9-millimeter?
SANTORO: Yes, I was.
POKART: Old enough to rob people?
SANTORO: Yes.
POKART: Old enough to be in the drug business?
SANTORO: Yes.
POKART: And you sold crack?
SANTORO: Yes.
POKART: And you know what crack does to people?
SANTORO: Yes.
POKART: Destroys people?
SANTORO: Yes.
POKART: That is OK with you?
SANTORO: I didn't force them to do it.

Pokart tried to make the jury ask themselves if Santoro might be lying to get a reduced sentence.

POKART: To get yourself out of jail you were willing to say and do anything, right?
SANTORO: Well, yes.
POKART: Including lying?
SANTORO: No, not lying.

Prosecutor Ray Marinaccio undermined this attack by pointing out that Santoro had identified Wright as the killer even before he was arrested for his part in the shoot-out.

After Santoro's testimony, Judge Figueroa wanted the case to go to the jury the next day. Outraged, Pokart explained that he needed at least one full day to call his witnesses and present his case.

"You're giving me one day while Mr. Marinaccio had two weeks," Pokart argued.

The judge insisted he would charge the jury the next day. *Charging the jury* means instructing the jury about points of law that must govern their actions as they deliberate.

"Your honor is being totally unfair to the defense," Pokart protested. "I'm not asking you for a week, six days, three days. I am asking you for one day. For you not to give me one day, I find extraordinary and shocking. A man goes to jail for forty years if I mess up."

Judge Figueroa finally relented, giving Pokart and Rosenfeld their extra day. They used it to review the witness testimony for weak spots in the prosecutor's case.

The judge then discussed the charge he would make to the jury. Pokart argued that the judge should tell the jurors that the evidence presented was indirect (no one actually saw Wright shoot Hernandez). He also asked the judge to tell the jury that Archie Samuels's statement to the police and grand jury about Wright shooting Hernandez could not be used as evidence. Pokart also wanted Judge Figueroa to tell the jury that it could not hold it against his client that he did not testify. The judge agreed.

As the law requires, the defense made its summation to the jury first. Steve Pokart explained that there are two main kinds of evidence—eyewitness and scientific. In this case, the prosecution offered only eyewitness testimony, which is the least reliable evidence. No scientific evidence linked the defendant to the shooting. The prosecution had not proved that the pistol used in the shooting belonged to his client or even that the weapon in evidence was the murder weapon.

Pokart then questioned the credibility of the prosecution's witnesses. Archie Samuels's testimony, he said, was unreliable because the police may have coerced him. Joseph Santoro's testimony was unreliable because it might have been offered in exchange for a reduced sentence. Pokart pointed out that neither witness claimed to have actually seen his client shoot Danny Hernandez.

Pokart then opened a brown paper bag and dramatically put ten White Owl cigars on the railing in front of the jury. Then he added two more. He asked the jury to imagine that each tobacco cigar contained marijuana. He went on to explain that some witnesses had smoked this much marijuana in addition to drinking large amounts of alcohol.

After the prosecution's summation, Judge Figueroa charged the jury. He explained that they must consider three charges: murder, reckless endangerment, and criminal possession of a gun. He said that it was their responsibility to review the testimony in order to determine the facts of the case. He explained what they could and could not consider as evidence. He again explained that Wright was presumed innocent and could not be convicted as long as the jury felt there was a reasonable doubt of his guilt.

The jury retired to deliberate. To everyone's surprise, they reached a verdict in a matter of hours. Wright watched the jury closely as the verdict was announced.

Wright was found not guilty on the murder charge and guilty on the charges of reckless endangerment and illegal possession of a weapon. Later, one of the jurors explained their decision and their reaction to Pokart and the defense team:

I thought Pokart did an excellent job of defending his client. He presented a spirited and energetic defense. He said something very important in his first presentation to the jury: "The prosecutor will present no eyewitnesses that saw Nat Wright shoot Danny Hernandez, nor will anyone present any scientific evidence that will connect his client to the gun that killed Danny." So when we went into the jury room, most of us had already concluded that the prosecutor never proved that Wright actually killed Danny, even though most of us felt that Wright was indeed the killer. But we could not convict him on what we felt.

The juror explained that on the first vote, the jury was seven to five for acquittal on the murder charge. However, the five in favor of conviction quickly agreed with the majority. All the jurors agreed there was sufficient evidence to prove Wright was the gunman who fired at Santoro.

Two months later, the judge sentenced Nat Wright to thirteen years. In a sense, Pokart's original advice to his client turned out to be correct. If Nat Wright had followed his advice, he would have gotten twelve years or less.

"I told him in the beginning that if we went to trial, he would see what a good lawyer I am—but he would lose the case. In a sense, that's what happened, even though he was acquitted of the charge of murder. He wound up with more time on the lesser charge than he would have had if he had pleaded guilty to the murder itself," Pokart said.

After his sentencing, Nat Wright thanked his attorneys and was escorted out of the courtroom to prison. Did he do the crime? And if he did, was justice served if he was not convicted of it?

"We'll never know what really happened," Rosenfeld said. "Unless the gunman, whoever he may be, decides to tell us."

 # DNA Goes to Court: The Acquittal of O. J. Simpson

While eyewitnesses are often unreliable, scientific evidence is supposed to be foolproof. The case described in this chapter focuses on the use of DNA evidence in the courtroom. In this case, an African-American football hero named O. J. Simpson was accused of murdering his ex-wife and her friend. The prosecution claimed it had irrefutable scientific evidence proving Simpson's guilt. DNA testing seemed to prove that Simpson's blood was connected to the scene of the crime. To win the case, Simpson's legal team had to challenge the validity of the evidence.

Johnnie L. Cochran Jr. is a well-known African-American lawyer. The grandson of a Louisiana sharecropper, he worked his way up through Loyola Law School to become one of Hollywood's most prominent lawyers. Another prominent African-American whose life began modestly was O. J. Simpson, a legendary football great with the Buffalo Bills. After being charged with murdering his ex-wife, Nicole Brown Simpson, and her friend, Ronald Goldman, Simpson hired a legal team that included Johnnie Cochran to represent him.

The details of the case are almost common knowledge. On the evening of June 12, 1994, Nicole Brown Simpson returned home to discover that her mother left her sunglasses at a restaurant where they had just had dinner. She called the restaurant and asked if someone could deliver the glasses to her house. A young waiter and friend named Ronald Goldman volunteered. When Goldman arrived, the two of them talked on the sidewalk for several minutes. Suddenly a person or persons with a knife brutally attacked and killed them both.

When the police arrived, they realized that Nicole Brown Simpson was O. J. Simpson's ex-wife. One of the first detectives at the crime scene was Mark Fuhrman, a fifteen-year veteran of the Los Angeles Police Department (LAPD) homicide squad. Fuhrman discovered the notorious bloody glove at the scene of the crime and blood on O. J.'s white Ford Bronco. It was later shown that Fuhrman was deeply prejudiced against blacks.

The police began to leak reports to the public and the press that O. J. Simpson was the primary suspect. At the preliminary hearing, the prosecution put forward several incriminating facts. The bloody glove, allegedly Simpson's, contained fibers of Goldman's and Nicole Brown Simpson's hair. Bloodstained socks found in O. J. Simpson's bedroom also contained blood samples from both victims. The blood of Goldman, Nicole Brown Simpson, and O. J. Simpson was found in various locations at the crime scene, on O. J. Simpson's car, and in his house. Bloody shoeprints found at the scene were consistent with a special brand of shoe that O. J. Simpson wore. And Simpson had abused his wife before their divorce.

The police campaign had its effect on public opinion. Polls showed that most Americans believed Simpson was guilty.

Johnnie Cochran, who took on the case, pointed out the racial drama underlying the case:

This photo of a glove found at the scene was entered as evidence in the O. J. Simpson murder trial.

Race plays a part in everything. . . . We don't introduce that there are racial issues. The jurors know it. Everybody knows it. . . . Race plays a part of everything in America. Race was the issue. How, in a case where a black man and a white woman were [a couple]—in a country in which this was forbidden in almost every state of the Union for almost 300 years—can race not be an issue?

Race was certainly an issue when it came to Detective Mark Fuhrman, who had expressed deep hostility to African-Americans and had been videotaped using the term *nigger*. Cochran and his colleague, attorney Robert Shapiro, were confident that they could undermine Fuhrman's credibility by revealing his racism.

But of all the evidence that the prosecution presented, the main charge was O. J. Simpson's DNA at the crime scene. The state claimed that the blood samples found on O. J. Simpson's clothing, especially his socks, contained DNA from the two victims and that blood samples found at the crime scene were O. J. Simpson's. The claim, if true, was damning.

DNA is the acronym for deoxyribonucleic acid, genetic material that carries a set of instructions unique to each human being. DNA can be extracted from a person's blood, hair, skin, sperm, or tissue. It can be found on a postage stamp, broken glass, a car seat, or clothing.

Once extracted, scientists can examine DNA in a laboratory to reveal a pattern. That pattern can be compared to a sample taken from a suspect. If the patterns match, the odds are extremely high that the suspect was at the crime scene. However, room for doubt still exists

Defendant O. J. Simpson with his lawyers, Johnnie Cochran (left) and Robert Shapiro (right)

because the tests compare only a small number of the chemical units of a person's genetic heritage.

But by and large, most prosecutors and defense attorneys feel that DNA is almost foolproof. If the pattern fails to match, the odds are even higher that the person is not responsible for the crime. Ronald Allen, a professor of criminal law at Northwestern University, said in *Newsweek* (November 16, 1998), "DNA is more reliable than anything else we have—so long as you have a good sample and a competent lab following appropriate procedures. If those conditions are met, DNA evidence is devastating."

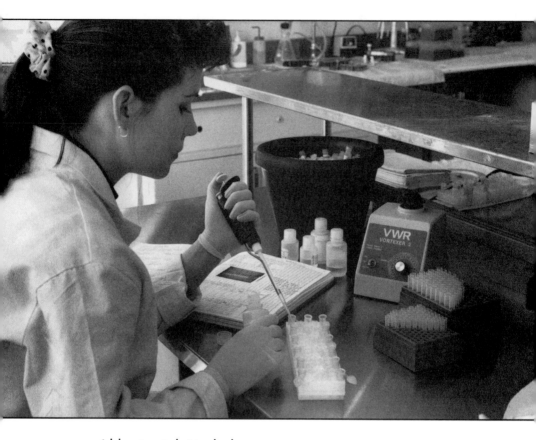

A laboratory technician loads
a gel for DNA analysis.

DNA analysis

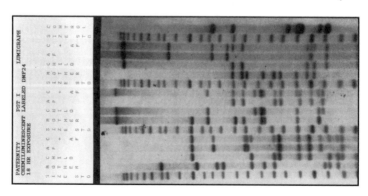

In high-profile cases with attorneys whose fees run into millions of dollars, the defense must examine every possible argument that the prosecution might present. It must hire private investigators, jury advisers, and blood analysis and DNA experts. To counter the claim that DNA samples found at the murder scene and on Simpson's clothing proved he was guilty, Cochran and Shapiro brought in two top lawyers in the field of DNA defense—Barry Scheck and Peter Neufeld.

Scheck and Neufeld were experts in using DNA to prove innocence. In 1991, Scheck and Neufeld established the Innocence Project at the Benjamin R. Cardozo School of Law, where Scheck is a teacher. Scheck, Neufeld, and other lawyers began to solicit requests from prisoners who felt that DNA evidence could prove them innocent. The only requirement was that biological evidence, such as semen in a rape case or hair or skin in a murder case, remained. The defense lawyers then ran tests to see if the DNA samples contained in the evidence matched their client's.

Incredibly, the tests revealed that the DNA from crime scenes did not match 60 percent of their clients—sixty-seven cases at the time of writing. That is, there was an extremely high probability that the prisoners were innocent of crimes for which they had already served many years in jail. After DNA evidence was presented in the courtroom, many convictions were overturned. Unfortunately, the legal process to get DNA evidence reexamined in court can take many years. As a result, some wrongfully imprisoned defendants never get a rehearing.

Simpson's defense team knew the samples had to be handled with extreme care in order for the DNA results to be valid. It was their job to show that the testing on Simpson's blood had been compromised by the Los Angeles Police Department.

The defense team began with police videotapes of the crime scene, especially footage showing how the blood samples were collected. They discovered that LAPD lab technicians Dennis Fung and Andrea Mazzola collected evidence with their bare hands, put blood samples inside a plastic bag, and stored them in an unrefrigerated van for twelve hours. They also discovered that one police officer carried a blood sample in his pocket for three hours before taking it to the lab.

Prosecutors claimed that a blood sample from a

Defense attorneys Peter Neufeld (left) and Barry Scheck examine DNA evidence in the O. J. Simpson trial.

back gate at the crime scene had high levels of O. J. Simpson's DNA. That sample had not been found until several weeks after the murders, however. Scheck and Neufeld pointed out that later tests showed that blood samples from the gate and the sock had samples of EDFT, a chemical used to prevent blood clotting. This suggested that the blood supposedly found at the crime scene actually came from a test tube of blood that Simpson had supplied police voluntarily. Scheck and Neufeld also pointed out that the samples had high levels of Simpson's DNA, which was unlikely after three weeks had passed. The defense team used these facts to plant in the jury's minds the idea that blood was planted at the crime scene to "prove" Simpson's guilt.

By emphasizing the mishandling of the DNA evidence, Scheck and Neufeld were able to neutralize the prosecution's strongest argument. Combined with the rest of the defense team's evidence that Detective Fuhrman was a racist, it raised a reasonable doubt in the jury's minds.

The strategy was effective. Although several jurors later said that they felt Simpson was guilty, they believed the defense attorneys had challenged the prosecution's evidence successfully. They felt they had to find Simpson not guilty, because the case against him had not been proven beyond a reasonable doubt.

The trial lasted 265 days. Nineteen different lawyers were involved in the case. More than 100 witnesses were called. Some 488 exhibits were submitted, and 34,500 pages of transcripts were generated. The case caused mass-media hysteria for almost two years, polarized racial relations in America, and left millions of Americans believing that Simpson got away with a double murder because he had the money for the best team of defense lawyers.

Would O. J. Simpson have been found not guilty if he had been poor? It is highly doubtful. While Simpson might have found skilled and dedicated public defenders to represent him, he would not have been able to afford experts and investigators. Many poor defendants have excellent attorneys but no financial resources to hire experts. As a result, innocent people are sometimes convicted of crimes they did not commit and spend years in prison.

THREE

 # Terror on Trial

In the case described in this chapter, defense attorney Lynne Stewart represented Sheik Omar Abdel-Rahman. Rahman was a blind Muslim cleric (religious leader) accused of leading an Islamic terrorist group that planned to bomb New York City. Since there was no evidence that the sheik had actually planned or organized the bombings or committed any terrorist acts, Stewart believed the case would rest on the issue of free speech.

During lunch hour in lower Manhattan's busy financial district on February 26, 1993, men and women bundled in overcoats piled into waiting elevators in some of the world's tallest buildings. From the observation deck of the twin towers of the 110-story World Trade Center, tourists marveled at the Statue of Liberty in the harbor as freighters and tankers from around the world sailed by.

On the snow-covered streets below, frustrated truck drivers and cabbies stuck in traffic leaned on their horns. Pedestrians crossed the streets, weaving in and out of the stalled traffic. A Ryder rental van slid away from the traffic, easing down the ramp of the World Trade Center. The van cruised around the lower basement until the driver found a parking spot against a wall. Behind the wall stood one-fourth of the building's support columns. The driver parked and left quickly.

Fifteen minutes later, a 1,500-pound (680-kg) bomb inside the van exploded with cataclysmic force, blowing the garage to pieces and causing unimaginable chaos. The explosion created a "cyclone-force wind" moving 5,000 feet (1,525 m) per second, pulverizing cars, reducing cinderblock walls to dust, and sending a 14,000-pound (6,350-kg) steel beam flying through space like an arrow. The 11-inch (28-cm) thick, steel-reinforced concrete slab beneath the van disintegrated into a heap of dust. A deadly plume of soot and smoke shot 1/4 mile (0.4 km) high, into the elevator shafts, stairwells, and ventilation system. Six people were killed and more than 1,000 were injured.

Headlines screamed that terrorism had come to America. Within two days, investigators discovered a vehicle identification number in the rubble that allowed them to trace the vehicle to the Ryder rental agency. On March 4, 1993, the Federal Bureau of Investigation (FBI) arrested Mohammed Salameh, an Egyptian national. Shortly afterward, three other men were arrested. In 1995, all were tried and convicted for the bombing.

During the trial, the press seized on the fact that

Emergency vehicles surround the twin towers of the World Trade Center after the bombing on February 26, 1993.

Police escort an injured woman from the World Trade Center.

several of the defendants worshiped at a mosque in Jersey City, New Jersey, where Sheik Omar Abdel-Rahman regularly preached. Sheik Rahman, blind and living in exile, fled from Egypt because he was opposed to the regime of Hosni Mubarak, Egypt's president. In Egypt, Sheik Rahman had been charged with plotting to assassinate Mubarak but was found not guilty. In

Sheik Omar Abdel-Rahman alone in his cell during trial

America, he called publicly for Mubarak's death and the overthrow of Egypt's government to set up an Islamic state.

In June 1993, agents from the FBI raided a "bomb factory" in Queens, a borough of New York City. They found several men in the act of mixing diesel fuel and fertilizer in a garage. Their plan was to set off twelve bombs throughout New York City at six highly populated locations, including the Statue of Liberty, Grand Central Station, and Times Square. The plot was discovered on a hidden video and audiotape.

By the time the arrests took place, some fifteen men, including Sheik Rahman, were in jail. Although there was no clear evidence linking Sheik Rahman with the bomb plots, the state charged that he was the spiritual leader of the plot and gave the conspirators religious sanction for their actions.

After Sheik Rahman's arrest, one of the attorneys for the other defendants asked Lynne Stewart to defend Sheik Rahman. Stewart has made a career of defending unpopular clients, including political radicals, drug dealers, and criminals who resist the police. She has been characterized by one newspaper reporter as "a counselor at law and a radical at heart." "Perhaps," she says with tongue in cheek, "it's because I like to carry a purple tote bag and wear a New York Mets cap."

Actually she takes pride in having a number of clients she considers to be revolutionaries—willing to stand up against economic and racial injustice in America. Stewart says there was nothing in her conservative, Protestant upbringing that indicated her future legal career. What she remembers most about her youth was how difficult it was for a teenage girl to be smart in the 1950s:

I once said to my mother, "All my friends have boyfriends and I don't have a boyfriend, and what's the matter with me?" Expecting my wonderful mother to say, "Nothing's the matter with you! They're jerks, they're stupid, they'll grow up." Instead she said, "Well maybe you shouldn't act so smart all of the time. Dumb down, in other words, so you don't put them off by being so smart." I still remember that like it was yesterday! It was so amazing to me that my mother would say this to me! But that was symptomatic of the era. That was what it was like, and it was painful.

In the 1960s, Stewart became a teacher. She wanted to provide a quality education for black and Hispanic children. But she found the system bureaucratic, gave up teaching, and enrolled in law school. Her interest was criminal law, in part because she mistrusted the fairness of the criminal justice system. In law school, she was influenced by two of America's most outstanding civil rights lawyers, William Kunstler and Ernest Kinoy.

Stewart quickly got a reputation for defending the underdog. Many of her clients began to refer her to others. "Even," she says laughingly, "when they lost their case and went to jail."

Sometimes she will take on a client if the case interests her politically. If the client agrees, she has offered to work pro bono.

Lynne Stewart met Sheik Rahman after his arrest and they hit it off. Even though she liked him, she felt she did not have sufficient time to prepare his defense. "I'm a preparation freak. When I go to trial I have to have every piece of paper cataloged where I can find it. I have to know the case backward and forward."

She told her colleagues she couldn't do it. One of them replied, "Lynne, if there's a building burning and you see a baby inside, you don't say I haven't time to put my boots and fireproof coat on. You run in there and get that baby out of the building. Even if you can't do it the way you think it should be done." She took the case.

Stewart felt that Sheik Rahman was difficult to defend because of deep anti-Muslim sentiment in America. While she believed the evidence against him was weak, she knew prejudice against him was strong.

I spoke to my brother-in-law, who happens to be Jewish. "Well, what do you think about the sheik's case?" I said. And he said, "When I look at him I feel like he's someone who should be in jail for the rest of his life." "Without hearing anything?" I asked. And he said, "That's my visceral reaction." So I knew going into it that this must be the reaction of most Americans. At one point I said, in arguing with the judge about whether I should be allowed to speak to the press, "If you stop people at random walking down Centre Street, I guarantee you that ten out of ten, if I say 'Muslim' they'll say 'terrorist.' So, I said, 'That's what we're up against, and they've had two years to do publicity and the sheik hasn't had the chance to do any because he's never had a spokesperson. So when the press is out there with those cameras, I'm going to speak.'"

Stewart was aware that her client looked like a stereotypical terrorist in part because he wears dark glasses to cover his blind eyes. "One of the things I did very early in the case was to ask him, 'Sheik, why do you

54

wear dark glasses?' " He said he was told to do that because his eyes frighten people.

"No," I said. "The glasses make you look sinister. It makes you look like what they say you are, evil incarnate. It's better to see no eyes than those glasses."

Since Sheik Rahman did not speak English, Stewart became his voice to the public. She felt that to win the case, she must also fight in the court of public opinion. On the first day of the trial, she held a press conference on the steps of the courthouse. She claimed that the issue is one of free speech. "The evidence is purely what he said, what he preached, what he thought," she argued.

Later, the trial judge challenged her interpretation in court. He told the jury "no man is charged here with having opinions or expressing opinions, which in this country is not a crime."

The prosecution built its case around the unusual charge of seditious conspiracy. Seditious conspiracy is an obscure nineteenth-century law that makes it a crime to "conspire to overthrow or put down, or destroy by force the government of the United States." Enacted after the Civil War, the law was for use against Southerners who rejected the authority of the federal government. Later, it was used against socialists and communists. In this case, the prosecution claimed that a wide conspiracy existed to launch a campaign of terror and murder against the American people.

The defendants were accused of conspiring to "levy a war of urban terrorism against the United States." Prosecutors charged that the attack on the World Trade Center was part of an overall conspiracy to intimidate

Lynne Stewart (right) addresses the press in the Sheik Omar Abdel-Rahman case, charging that he was arrested for exercising his right to free speech.

the United States into changing Middle East policies favoring Israeli and Egyptian governments.

By charging Sheik Rahman with seditious conspiracy, all the government had to prove was that he *intended* to wage a campaign against the United States. He did not have to commit a specific crime to be found guilty.

Stewart argued that the law's broadness allows people to be prosecuted for their political or religious beliefs— or for statements that don't really reflect an intent to commit a crime.

"The charge of seditious conspiracy has never been used successfully against an American citizen born in this country," she said, "because of our roots, because of where we come from. This is our great tradition. American juries have seldom convicted people of sedition."

Lynne Stewart felt the jury would be sympathetic to her client because it was ethnically mixed: "I thought they were people who would understand what it is to have the finger pointed at you just because you are a black or a Latino. And so they would understand when I point out that my client was arrested because he is a Muslim."

In her opening argument, Stewart argued that her client was on trial for his militancy and not for any overt action: "The evidence will show you that his case is before you not because of anything he did. He is, after all, elderly, blind, diabetic, with a heart condition. The evidence will show you that he is charged based solely on his words, words uttered as part of his duties as a Muslim cleric, words uttered as religious teachings, words protected under our Constitution."

Stewart pointed out that, in July 1993, U.S. attorney general Janet Reno told then-U.S. senator from New York Al D'Amato that there was not enough evidence to charge Sheik Rahman. "Yet two months later, with nothing new developing, he is charged. He is indicted," Stewart said. "And not merely charged, he is charged as the leader, the head man, the person responsible for everything. Why?"

Stewart's answer was that the U.S. government wanted to do the Egyptian government a favor: "They put Dr. Abdel-Rahman in this case. Did he disagree with U.S. policy? He did. Did he conspire, seditiously or otherwise? He did not."

She claimed that her client was a charismatic, respected religious leader who did nothing more than use his right to free speech to agitate for the overthrow of a government he believed was oppressing its people. She claimed that Sheik Rahman was the victim of a trumped-up case, set up by an informant with a history of lying.

The informant was Emad Ali Salem, an Egyptian who worked for the FBI. The government admitted that Salem was paid $1,056,200 for his testimony and placed in a witness-protection program. They also revealed that the FBI had once dismissed Salem because he failed a lie-detector test. After the World Trade Center bombing, he was rehired. Salem had infiltrated the bomb plot and made hundreds of secret tapes of the conspirators.

Sheik Rahman's biggest problem was a taped conversation he had with Salem. On the tape, Salem tried to trap Sheik Rahman by getting his blessing to commit violent acts. Salem suggested they blow up the United Nations building. Sheik Rahman said not to do that because even if it was not religiously incorrect, it would be bad for Muslims. Sheik Rahman also told Salem not to blow up the United Nations. While Sheik Rahman did not condemn Salem's plan, he never urged the bombing of any building. He did suggest that Salem

In this courtroom artist's sketch, Lynne Stewart and Sheik Omar Abdel-Rahman listen to the testimony of Emad Ali Salem, the chief prosecution witness.

should find a way "to inflict damage on the United States Army."

When it was time to examine Salem on the witness stand, Stewart knew she must paint him as a liar whose goal was to entrap her client.

STEWART: Did you lie to federal agents that you were once in Egyptian intelligence?

SALEM: Yes.

STEWART: That you knew several leaders of Arab governments?

SALEM: Yes.

STEWART: Did you lie about your marriage to an American woman to get your citizenship?

SALEM: Yes.

STEWART: When you swore loyalty to the United States in this very courthouse, was that true or a lie as well?

SALEM: It was true. . . . I tried to maintain myself to be a big shot.

Stewart tried to call expert witnesses about the faith of Islam to prove that Sheik Rahman's views were not on the radical fringe. The judge ruled against her efforts. She did tell the jury that Sheik Rahman spoke out against Egypt and America's support because he felt that he could do so in America. Later she explained:

The judge refused to allow us to bring in experts. So we must have put thirty people on the witness stand from different mosques, from all walks of life, saying they had heard the sheik preach a hundred times and never heard him urge violence, never heard him say "Tear down America, blow up America, kill Americans." He urged them to fight jihad *[holy war], but he urged them to go to Bosnia, to Afghanistan and fight with the forces there. So we did all of that, undermining perhaps some of the witnesses the government had put on, and putting the lie to some other things. And when I summed up the case for two days in front of the jury, I really had a very good feeling about the outcome. I felt that this jury had been there for nine months, they had seen him every day and would acquit him.*

The trial took its toll on Stewart. "It's probably the most exhausting work you can do. You work in court from ten to five and then go home and work seven to midnight and then go back to court the next day," Stewart said. "And when you're in court, you must be on your toes every minute because you can't afford not to pay close attention. Sometimes I feel that I can't do this anymore and that I'm losing my edge. But once I step into the courtroom, I'm okay."

In her closing argument to the jury, Stewart emphasized that the main evidence against her client was the word of an informant, a man she characterized as a "hyena." "There is really something that stinks about law enforcement targeting a person for prosecution when a world power like the United States can be manipulated by a person like Emad Salem," she said.

Stewart misread the jury. After almost three weeks of deliberation, it found all of the defendants guilty of forty-eight of fifty charges. While the others were sentenced to twenty-five to seventy-five years, Sheik Rahman was given life in prison without parole.

Sheik Rahman was defiant. He gave a 100-minute speech in Arabic condemning the United States as the enemy of Islam and God and called the trial unlawful.

Lynne Stewart was bitterly disappointed by the outcome of the trial. She explained:

I think after the World Trade Center bombing, people became frightened. The prosecutor said in his summation a point which I vigorously objected to—he said, "Americans [have] the right to be free from fear. And these people wanted to take that away from you when they plotted to blow up these landmarks." I think this played on the prejudices of the jury to make them feel that they would be happier with those guys in jail.

I really feel in this case the government had a political agenda, and part of their political agenda was to make sure that Egypt remained their ally. And the sheik was really capable of disturbing that. He was capable of having Egypt, which is America's main bulwark and the most powerful country in the Middle East, go over to being at least neutral, if not being on the other side. They had to stop him somehow. And so they did. . . . He's not the first person to go to prison for his beliefs and he won't be the last.

Almost two years after the trial, the federal district court denied Lynne Stewart's appeal to overturn the verdict.

FOUR

Inside Family Court

When children are accused of crimes, the defense attorney's responsibility often goes beyond mounting a defense in court. If the client is convicted, the attorney works to help the child escape harsh punishment from the law and receive psychological counseling or other needed social services. In the case described in this chapter, attorney Traci Douglas was convinced her ten-year-old client was not guilty of sexually assaulting a classmate. However, she was prepared to get him into a therapeutic program if he was found guilty.

Vernon was listening to his teacher explain the great civilization of ancient Egypt when the assistant principal entered the classroom and whispered something to the teacher. The teacher then turned to Vernon and instructed him to go to the principal's office. Several of his classmates giggled. Everyone wondered what kind of trouble Vernon was in now.

Only ten years old, Vernon had been suspended from school several times for fighting, disrupting classes, and harassing other students. The only person surprised that Vernon had been summoned to the principal's office was Vernon himself.

When Vernon entered the principal's office, two men sat with the visibly upset principal. She informed Vernon that he would be arrested and that his mother was on her way to the school. Vernon would be taken to the police station. Later, the principal would say, "I have never had a pupil in my school arrested until Vernon. But then, I've never had a child like Vernon either."

At the police station, Vernon was charged with sexually abusing a female classmate. He was accused of touching her "private areas" when the two were playing together in the schoolyard. The complaint was made several months after the alleged incident occurred. Vernon was fingerprinted, photographed, and booked. Since the charge was a serious crime, or felony, he could be sent to a detention center for children until the age of eighteen. After he was booked, the police issued a summons for Vernon to appear in family court and released him into his mother's custody.

Vernon's desperate mother contacted the Neighborhood Defender Service. A nonprofit, community-based legal services society in Harlem, New York, the Neighborhood Defender Service represents local residents free of charge. People who are in trouble with the law can walk in off the street and receive free legal assistance. The city and state government and various foundations fund the organization.

Traci Douglas discusses a case with Leonard Noisette, director of the Neighborhood Defender Service.

Vernon and his mother met with Traci Douglas, a tall young African-American graduate of Harvard Law School. In law school, Douglas once interned for a corporate law firm. The experience convinced her not to enter corporate law. "I came to the conclusion that what I wanted to do with my life is help people who are caught up in the criminal justice system, especially young people who often get in trouble because they lack survival skills for today's society," she said. When people sometimes ask her, "How can you defend those [guilty] people?" Douglas replies:

People are often appalled by the crimes my clients commit. I don't justify what they have done, but I don't condemn them either. Children who grow up in the streets of poor neighborhoods often have to live by different rules to survive. I can't tell children how they should live when every day is a harsh struggle for survival. I try to help them get in programs that will improve their lives and try to get jobs for their mothers. But I can't condemn them if they fail.

Vernon impressed Douglas the first time she met him. "I'll never forget the first time I saw Vernon. I thought to myself, 'there is no way this child could have

Traci Douglas works for children accused of crimes.

been involved in the crime.' He was innocent looking, about 4 feet [120 cm] tall and very cute. His mother was about twenty-five, but she looked older. Her face was hard and revealed that she had had a tough life." But Douglas knew that innocent looks are no proof of innocence.

Douglas explained to Vernon's mother that the case would be heard in family court, not criminal court. Family court is designed for young people who are legally minors, usually sixteen years old and younger. If a child commits a crime, he is considered a juvenile delinquent rather than a person criminally responsible. In most states, a juvenile delinquent is between seven and sixteen years old. Some states, such as New York, have lowered the age to thirteen for adult prosecution for serious crimes, violent felonies, or murder. However, sentencing is usually lighter than for adults.

The rules of family court differ from those of criminal court. There is no jury. Instead, a family court judge determines guilt or innocence in a fact-finding hearing. The defendant is called a respondent. The defense attorney is considered a law guardian, not a lawyer. During the hearing, the prosecution and defense present their cases and call witnesses. In family court, judges are limited in sentencing by law.

Because Vernon is ten, the maximum sentence he can receive is eighteen months in a secured juvenile facility. However, the facility can petition the court to hold him until he is eighteen years old if it believes he should remain.

As Douglas investigated Vernon's case, she continued to handle a variety of cases. On a typical day, she may rush back and forth from family court to criminal

A judge renders a verdict in family court, where there is no jury.

court. When one client didn't show up for his hearing, Douglas tried to track him down by phone—without success. Another client arrested on drug charges begged Douglas to convince the judge to release her from detention. The judge denied the request because it was the second time in six months this person had been arrested for dealing drugs. After Douglas found a drug program that would accept her client, the judge agreed to release her if she pleaded guilty and accepted probation. A third client was arrested for slapping and kicking her nine-year-old nephew in an elevator. Although she denied kicking the child, she pleaded guilty and accepted probation rather than face a trial in which the main witness against her was a social worker.

Between work on these cases, Douglas attempted to reach the parents of children who knew both Vernon and the child he was accused of assaulting, Samantha. She hoped she might find a weakness in Samantha's charges. However, the parents refused to allow their children to talk to her. Douglas was not surprised: "It is understandable that they don't want to get involved, but at the same time it's frustrating. Even if their children don't testify in court, at least they could give me information that I could use to help Vernon."

While waiting for Vernon's hearing, Douglas managed to get him transferred to a special school in his neighborhood. She sees this as part of her job as a community lawyer. After several weeks, Vernon had trouble at the special school. He wanted to go shopping with his mother at 3 P.M., but the teacher wouldn't let him leave class until 3:30 P.M. Furious, he began to throw things around the room. Although he did not physically attack his teacher, she reported that she was frightened of him and couldn't control him.

Douglas tried to get Vernon to understand that he was making his situation worse by acting out that way. Vernon promised to do better. "But I also knew that there were times he did the things he did because he couldn't control himself," Douglas said later.

As the date for the hearing neared, Douglas decided to put Vernon on the witness stand even though it is not required. She prepared Vernon for his appearance. She was careful not to put words in his mouth. At the same time, she had to help him give a clear account of what happened.

To convince the judge that there was a reasonable doubt that Vernon was guilty, Douglas knew she had to undermine Samantha's credibility. She believed Samantha was lying. She believed Samantha had engaged in sexual encounters with several boys. Vernon told Douglas that boys had said Samantha had invited them to her home and watched X-rated movies with them when her parents were not there.

Challenging a child's credibility without hard evidence can backfire, however. Children often tend to distort reality on a witness stand. If the child begins to cry during questioning, the judge could hold it against the attorney and find the young respondent guilty. Douglas was also worried about Vernon being sent to a residential facility away from home. She thought being separated from his mother at such a young age would have tragic consequences.

On the day of the trial, Douglas met Vernon and his mother in the large waiting area in the family court. There are a number of courtrooms on the floor. Thirty or more cases are heard each day in each courtroom. Not all cases involve serious crimes. Family court hears cases about domestic violence, visiting rights, child abuse, foster care, and adoption.

Most juvenile offenders are, like Vernon, released into the custody of their parents until their case is settled. But some are held in detention because serious charges have been brought against them or they have no relatives to look after them. Vernon was shocked to see the tough, hardened look of young people who have experienced the worst that life has to offer.

70

As people waited for their case to be called, a sense of gloom and despair hung over the room. Many people sat silently with their heads bowed. A few wept. Mothers told their children how to answer when the judge questioned them. "Be polite. Say 'sir.' Or 'your honor' . . . that's even better." "Tell the truth—that you was only the lookout and it was the other kids who broke into the house."

Television personality Judge Judith Sheindlin was a family court judge for many years. She is acutely aware of the sadness of family court: "What keeps us in busi-

Judge Judith Sheindlin presiding in family court. Unless the crime is a particularly violent one, criminal cases involving defendants under sixteen are tried in family court.

ness in family court is a pervasive hopelessness. Most of the young people we see believe that they're never going to have a kind of lifestyle where they have job opportunities, have a nice home, drive a car, take a vacation. There is a hopelessness that family court cannot do anything about."

During Vernon's hearing, only Vernon and Samantha would testify. Because Vernon would take the stand, Douglas warned him that the prosecutor would question him about his bad behavior in school. Douglas's goal was to show that Vernon and his accuser had been friends for over a year and that no incidents had ever occurred between them. Douglas wanted to show the judge that whatever Vernon might have done in class, he would never have done anything to harm a friend.

DOUGLAS: Was Samantha in your class last year?
VERNON: Yes.
DOUGLAS: And how often did you see her?
VERNON: Every day.
DOUGLAS: Did you have the same lunch period every day?
VERNON: Yes.
DOUGLAS: Did you play together during lunch?
VERNON: Yes.
DOUGLAS: Were you still friends when the school year ended?
VERNON: Yes.
DOUGLAS: Did you see Samantha over the summer?
VERNON: Once or twice, but we didn't play together.
DOUGLAS: When this school year started, did you play in the yard during the same lunch period?

VERNON: Yes.

DOUGLAS: Do you remember what happened on the second day of school?

VERNON: The girl and her friends were playing jump rope and when it wasn't her turn, she sat down. I went over to say "hi" and put my arm around her and said, "Ooo baby."

DOUGLAS: What did you mean when you said "Ooo baby"?

VERNON: I don't know. I heard Tim the Tool Man say that to his wife [on *Home Improvement*]. But I didn't know what it meant.

DOUGLAS: Did you touch Samantha anywhere else but on the shoulder?

VERNON: No.

After Douglas questioned Vernon, the prosecutor cross-examined him. She brought out his history of getting into serious trouble in school. Then Samantha gave her version of the story, saying that when Vernon sat next to her, he touched her in an intimate place. Douglas then tried to undermine her credibility without challenging her directly.

DOUGLAS: You understand that court is different from school?

SAMANTHA: Yes.

DOUGLAS: And you understand that you are in court?

SAMANTHA: Yes.

DOUGLAS: And that you have to be honest about what happened and tell the truth now even if you didn't tell your mother or the prosecutor the truth before?

SAMANTHA: Yes.

DOUGLAS: You and Vernon played together, isn't that right?

SAMANTHA: Yes.

DOUGLAS: In fact, you played together the whole school year?

SAMANTHA: Yes.

DOUGLAS: He was nice to you and you were nice to him?

SAMANTHA: Yes.

DOUGLAS: You didn't fight with him and he didn't fight with you?

SAMANTHA: Yes.

Then Douglas began the tricky part of her examination. She wanted to get Samantha to admit that she invited boys over to her house when her parents were not home.

DOUGLAS: And sometimes you asked him to come over after school?

SAMANTHA: No, I didn't do that.

DOUGLAS: You asked him to come over because your parents weren't home?

SAMANTHA: No.

DOUGLAS: When you asked him, he didn't come over?

SAMANTHA: No.

DOUGLAS: And every time you asked him to come over he said no?

SAMANTHA: I never asked him to come over.

DOUGLAS: And you sometimes asked other boys to come over?

SAMANTHA: No, that's not true.

74

DOUGLAS: And when you asked them, they said yes and
                came over?
SAMANTHA: No!
DOUGLAS: But when you asked Vernon he said no.

At this point, Samantha began to cry. It wasn't clear if she was crying because she felt pressure from Douglas or she felt guilty for lying. Whatever her emotion, her story remained the same. Douglas's defense was hindered by her inability to find any classmates willing to verify Samantha's behavior with other boys.

The judge ultimately found Vernon guilty. Douglas was not surprised. "Samantha did very well on the witness stand," Douglas said. "She was well rehearsed. And we couldn't bring in any witnesses who could contradict her story. This, plus the fact that Vernon had such a bad record in school, worked against him."

The judge then asked for the probation department to investigate Vernon's history and make a recommendation about what to do. "What fascinated me," Douglas recalled, "was that once Vernon was found guilty, it seemed as if a great burden had been lifted off his shoulders. He began to do better in school. His teacher, who once reported she was afraid of him, was now giving him excellent reports."

Douglas then tried to get Vernon into a special program. She considers it her job to help her clients rebuild their lives in addition to representing them in court. So she tries to get them counseling and job training.

Although Vernon's behavior in school had improved, the probation department concluded that Vernon had severe discipline problems. The mental health report was also negative. The probation department recommended continued close supervision at a facility.

Traci Douglas fought to keep him in his own community. "We didn't want him placed upstate in a facility. If that happened, he would really be lost," she said. Douglas tried to find an agency that would work with Vernon while he lived at home. She got his case reviewed by the Juvenile Intensive Supervision Program (JISP), an agency in the probation department. JISP was Vernon's last hope to remain in his community.

Although Douglas was able to persuade the agency to take Vernon, the battle was not over. She still had to convince the judge to let Vernon enter the program. To win the judge over, Douglas gained the prosecutor's support for the plan. When the time came for sentencing, the judge gave Vernon permission to enter JISP—with a stern warning about following its rules.

Douglas's job was not yet finished. She felt that if Vernon's mother had a job, her relationship with Vernon would improve. So she helped her find a job as a home health aide.

Six months after the hearing, Douglas was pleased with the results:

The reports have all been good so far. Vernon is doing well in his new school. Through the JISP program, he is involved in programs in the local YMCA and boys' club. He is getting counseling and most importantly, he is working things out with his mother. I was able to help her get a job as a home health aide. So even though we lost the battle at the hearing, we are winning the fight to save Vernon's life from being destroyed. But it's always one day at a time.

FIVE

Incompetence on Death Row

When all legal remedies are exhausted, the
only hope left for a defendant, especially one
on death row, is a pardon or a commutation
of sentence by the state governor or a special
board. In the case described in this chapter,
Arkansas attorney John Jewell made a desperate bid to save his African-American client,
Ricky Ray Rector, from death despite hostile
public opinion and a governor's presidential
ambitions. A commutation is a reduction of
a sentence, usually from a death sentence
to life in prison with or without parole. A
pardon is an official statement ending the
penalty imposed upon someone for a crime.
But, as John Jewell found out, commuting a
sentence can often be a political rather than a
legal issue.

78

Ricky Ray Rector was born in the poor section of Conway, Arkansas, a college town about an hour northwest of Little Rock. He was one of seven children in a hardworking family. While most of his brothers and sisters grew up to lead productive lives, Ricky Ray Rector was different. He always played by himself. Lost in his own world, he was unable to connect with most people.

Ricky Ray Rector's mother tried to protect him. His father thought his son needed discipline and often whipped him, making the situation worse. A sister later described him as "a troubled child" to reporter Marshall Frady (*The New Yorker*, February 22, 1992): "He was having a hard life even then, and we just didn't know what it was, that he needed special attention. But he always had trouble because of it."

Ricky Ray Rector did poorly in school. In high school, he got into fights continually. Most of his classmates were frightened of him and avoided him. He eventually dropped out of school, took to the streets, and did odd jobs. He also began to attract attention from the police. Over time, he was charged with assault and battery, intent to kill, forgery, and grand larceny. All charges were eventually dismissed.

In 1981, at the age of twenty-nine, Ricky Ray Rector finally snapped. He and two friends went to a dance. When one of his friends was refused admission because he didn't have the three-dollar entrance fee, Ricky Ray Rector pulled out a gun, wounded two men, and killed a third, Autor Criswell. For the next several months, Rector hid in alleys and fields.

Finally, Rector agreed to turn himself in to Bob

 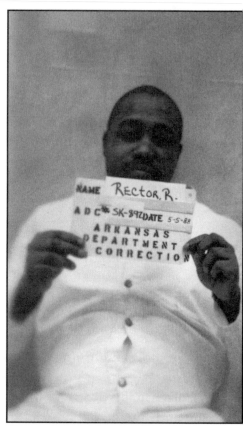

Ricky Ray Rector's police photographs

Martin, a white police officer. Officer Martin was regarded in the black community as a fair cop and considered a friend of the Rectors. When Martin arrived at Rector's house, he chatted with the family over a cup of coffee while waiting for Ricky Ray Rector to come downstairs. When Rector entered the kitchen, he greeted the officer and suddenly pulled out a .38-caliber pistol. He fired two shots into Martin's neck and jaw.

As his mother tried to help the dying officer, Ricky Ray Rector walked out of the house and told a relative he met, "I just shot that cop." Then he crossed the yard and put the gun to his head and pulled the trigger. The bullet moved through his skull, damaging brain tissues and his frontal lobes. Bullet fragments became lodged throughout his brain.

Ricky Ray Rector somehow survived the shooting, but lost much of his memory, the ability to concentrate, and the capacity to speak clearly. His eating habits changed, and his behavior grew bizarre. Often he just sat and stared. The doctors who operated on Ricky Ray Rector felt that he would probably end up in a mental institution for the rest of his life.

Instead, the state of Arkansas charged him with the murders of Autor Criswell (the man at the dance) and Officer Bob Martin. No one disputed that Rector had committed the murders. The key issue was whether he was competent to stand trial and be executed for his crimes.

Many of the people of Conway, including Bob Martin's family, felt that Rector had to pay for his crimes with his life, no matter what his mental capacity was. Whenever possible, politicians give the public what they want. Political careers can be made or lost on how closely public opinion is followed on death-penalty issues.

However, the Sixth Amendment to the Constitution requires that an accused person must be capable of meaningfully contributing to his defense. So, on September 28, 1981, Judge George Hartje held a six-hour hearing about Rector's mental competence. Psychiatric and medical experts testified for the defense and the prosecution. The defense specialists stated that Rector had a limited ability to understand what was said to him and a primitive understanding of death. His IQ was 63.

The prosecution experts, some of whom did not read Rector's medical reports until the day of the hearing, maintained that he was able to stand trial. Their arguments were often superficial and contradictory. Some experts for the prosecution accused Rector of faking his condition despite overwhelming physical and psychological evidence. Taking the conflicting testimony into account, Judge Hartje ruled with public opinion and found Rector competent to stand trial. One lawyer sarcastically remarked in private, "Judges also follow the election returns."

Two months later, Rector was tried and convicted of the murder of Autor Criswell. He was sentenced to life in prison without parole.

If the case had ended there, many people felt that justice would have been served. John Jewell, who served as Rector's attorney, noted, "If Ricky Ray [had been] allowed to live out his life, then he would have needed institutionalization until he died a natural death. Prison may not have been the best place for him, but, at least, he would have not been in a position to harm anyone anymore."

But the state of Arkansas did not leave the case there. A policeman had been killed and someone had to pay. Rector was tried for Bob Martin's death and convicted in fifteen minutes. An all-white jury then deliberated over the sentence—life in prison or the death penalty. Sixty minutes later, a death verdict was announced.

After the verdict was read, Ricky Ray Rector yawned. Later he asked, "Does this mean I'll get television in my cell now?"

It was at this point that the court appointed attorney John Jewell to handle Rector's federal appeal. Although Jewell's specialty was bankruptcy, he was familiar with the federal appeals process. However, it puzzled him that the court had chosen an attorney who had no criminal experience. Nevertheless, he was determined to do

John Jewell, the attorney who represented Ricky Ray Rector in the appeals process

whatever he could to keep Ricky Ray Rector from being executed.

Jewell had no doubt that Rector was mentally incompetent to be executed as well as stand trial. His task was to convince the Arkansas state courts or the federal courts that executing Rector violated his constitutional rights. He argued that since Rector was incapable of meaningfully assisting his attorney in his defense, the trial violated the Sixth Amendment. He also argued that executing a mentally incompetent person violated the Eighth Amendment, which prohibits the use of cruel and unusual punishment.

Jewell hoped that *Ford v. Wainwright,* a 1986 Supreme Court decision, might help. In that case, the Supreme Court ruled that anyone sentenced to execution must understand the fact that he has been condemned to die and the reason he has been sentenced to death.

Did Ricky Ray Rector meet these standards? Jewell and several psychologists maintained that Rector's understanding of death was like that of a child who understands that if you kill someone, you have to be punished. And psychologists at a federal facility in Missouri determined that although Rector had a basic understanding of the death penalty, he would "have considerable difficulty due to his organic defects in being able to work in a collaborative, cooperative effort with an attorney." In other words, Rector was mentally incapable of contributing to his own defense.

The Arkansas and federal district courts ducked Jewell's argument about Rector's mental competence. Instead they focused on Judge Hartje's decision that Rector was competent to stand trial. Since there was conflicting testimony at Rector's hearing about his mental state, the appeals court found that the Hartje decision was "entitled to a presumption of correctness." Thus the appeals court took the position that Ricky Ray Rector was mentally competent because a judge said he was. It did not matter to them whether Rector was mentally competent. The appeals court concluded as a matter of law—and not as a matter of fact—that Ricky Ray Rector knew he was to be executed and knew why he was to be executed. Neither of which, of course, was true.

As the legal debate continued, Rector's bizarre behavior continued. He ate incessantly and grew to almost 300 pounds (136 kg). At times, he hollered, danced, and shouted in his cell. At night, he sometimes acted like a scared child. Fearing someone would hurt him, he often cowered in his cell. He was terrified that alligators had been set loose in his cell.

In a final attempt to save Rector from execution, John Jewell asked a colleague, Jeff Rosenzweig, to file a claim in state court arguing that killing Rector would violate Arkansas law requiring inmates to be fit for execution. Jewell had Rosenzweig bring the challenge so that Jewell could testify about Rector's condition himself. If Jewell acted as Rector's legal representative, he would not be allowed to testify.

Jewell testified that Rector was incapable of having a serious conversation about his case, was obsessed with violence, and had no clear concept of death. Jewell pointed out that Rector continually referred to two fellow inmates, John Swindler and Gene Simmons, as if they were still alive, even though he knew they had been executed.

Jeff Rosenzweig, one of Ricky Ray Rector's attorneys

Jewell testified:

I found from my initial interview that he could respond affirmatively or agreeably to certain questions about his trial and the circumstances of the murders. But after maybe four or

five minutes, all communication broke down, and it became
merely a series of questions that are kind of, "What would you
do if somebody spit in your face?" "What would you do if
Swindler jumped you?" "Is Tommy Robinson bad?" "Is Little
Rock bad?" I met with him or talked with him fifteen times to
no avail. I had various frank conversations with him con-
cerning the fact that he will die and that he will be executed on
January 24. And each time it's like we're starting over and he
says, "Well, now what happens? Now what happens?" And I
say, "You're going to be executed on the 24th." I don't think he
has grasped the significance of the fact that he is to be execut-
ed. He shows no emotions. He maintains that Criswell (the
man he killed) is still alive. It is my opinion that he does not
grasp the significance of death, that he thinks he will be back
in his cell on Saturday morning.

Jewell and Rosenzweig also arranged for Frank
Parker, a fellow inmate on death row, to testify about his
experiences with Rector.

PARKER: No one can pass [Rector's] cell without
answering a long repertoire of questions
that he has about dogs. Mostly he howls.
He barks like a dog and especially at night I
have to shut him up and make him go to
bed. . . . The other inmates give him some
of their medication so that they can get
some sleep. Because if he's not sleeping,
he's howling, or let's say, like in the middle
of the night his light goes out, he'll start
screaming. He's afraid of the dark.

ROSENZWEIG: Have you ever had a deep conversation
with Mr. Rector?

PARKER: Rector has never had a deep conversation with anybody. He has no foothold on reality. He doesn't know what's going on most of the time. If somebody says something bad or something, Rector goes off trying to lug it up [trying to get one guy to jump another] or something.

ROSENZWEIG: In your opinion—obviously you are a lay person—is he competent?

PARKER: No . . . a garbage truck guy or anybody can tell you that Rector is not normal.

ROSENZWEIG: With regard to death and whether death is permanent?

PARKER: He thinks Swindler is still alive. He thinks his mother is still alive. He thinks they really don't execute you. They just make every-body think you're executed. He thinks Swindler is somewhere picking cotton. He thinks one of the cops or somebody he killed is still alive. He has no concept of death. He thinks when he dies, he's coming back.

ROSENZWEIG: Why do you testify on his behalf?

PARKER: I feel morally responsible, not for another human being because I don't think Rector is human. There are times I get mad at him and I'd choke him to death myself just to shut him up if I could. On death row, there's this feeling that you mind your business and I'll mind mine. Rector's case is none of my business but if I seen you attacking a retard-ed child, I'm going to get in it. Rector is not normal.

The prison building in Pine Bluff, Arkansas, that houses death-row inmates

The hearing made no impression on the court. It ruled that Rector was competent to be executed because Arkansas law did not cover the question of executing the insane. Since a federal judge already ruled that Rector could be executed, there were no legal remedies left to prevent the execution of Ricky Ray Rector.

Jewell's last chance to save Rector from death was

an appeal to Bill Clinton, who was governor of Arkansas at that time and had declared his candidacy for U.S. president. Clinton had asked the Arkansas parole board to review the case and make a recommendation to him.

The parole board is an independent body. But because the governor appoints its members, they often do what the governor wants. The two sides made their arguments at the hearing. Jewell rehearsed with Rector. "I coached Ricky what to say for two days. He was to ask for life imprisonment without parole rather than death," he said. Frank Parker also testified again.

While the board had been polite, Jewell felt it was more sympathetic to the family of the victims than to Rector. Bob Martin's wife and daughter strongly supported execution. "I'm not vengeful," Martin's wife said, "but I feel it's scriptural." The parole board did not recommend sparing Rector's life.

As Ricky Ray Rector's lawyers were fighting for his life, Bill Clinton was fighting for his own political future. He was under attack by a frenzied press. Former state employee Gennifer Flowers had publicly admitted to an affair with the Arkansas governor. Clinton's ratings suddenly dropped twelve points. He was on the ropes. Clinton was about to see his bid for the presidency crash. During this crisis, Clinton had to make his decision about Ricky Ray Rector's case.

Clinton knew what would happen if he commuted Rector's sentence to life without parole. In 1988, presidential candidate and Massachusetts governor Michael Dukakis suffered in the polls for allegedly authorizing the release of a black prisoner named Willy Horton who had gone on to commit brutal murder and rape.

The Republican Party ran television commercials accusing Dukakis of being soft on crime. Ironically, it was Dukakis's Republican predecessor who had authorized the release of Horton.

Of course, Ricky Ray Rector would never have been freed even if his sentence had been changed to life in prison. But Bill Clinton knew that a charge that he was soft on crime, combined with the Gennifer Flowers scandal, might have ended his presidential dream.

On death row, Rector watched Clinton on the television set outside his cell. John Jewell says that Rector told him, "Suppose it's true about him and all those women. Don't matter to me. I like him. I'm going to vote for him anyhow." Rector slept much of the day. Sometimes he called out the name "Cold Duck." No one was sure what he meant. At one point, it was reported, "He lay down on his bunk on his back and started what sounded like crying sounds."

January 24, 1992, was to be Ricky Ray Rector's last day on earth. He watched news reports about his execution on television. On one occasion, he laughed and clapped his hands during the report. The thought of death, lurking in his mind, came out in strange ways. Sometimes he told guards he was going home. Other times he said he would be executed but he would be asleep when it happened. He was heard shouting "No Mom! No Mom!" in his cell. He was impatient for his last meal—steak, fried chicken, beans, gravy, and pumpkin pie. As usual, he put his pie aside for later. "I'll finish it when I come back," he said.

John Jewell tried to get through to the governor, but Clinton's staff rebuffed him. He said, "They told me that he wasn't available to me." Jewell then asked some of Clinton's closest friends, including Jewell's fellow attorney, Jeff Rosenzweig, to speak to him on Rector's behalf. An old friend of Clinton's, Rosenzweig managed to finally reach the governor. He tried to convince Clinton that Rector was mentally a child. Although Clinton was sympathetic and seemed conflicted over Rector's execution, he was also determined not to intervene. Ricky Ray Rector would die on schedule.

"I hadn't thought much about the death penalty," Jewell later commented, "but now I see it's wrong. Our legal system is far too imperfect to execute people."

Shortly after 8 P.M., Rector dressed nervously in his white death suit—white shirt, pants, and socks. Seven guards escorted him into the death chamber. Meanwhile, thirteen witnesses to his death entered a viewing room separated from the death chamber by a glass window. John Jewell and Jeff Rosenzweig were two of the thirteen witnesses. Rector was hidden from sight behind a dark curtain. Like a theater audience, the witnesses waited for the curtain to rise and the drama to begin.

Ricky Ray Rector's execution was scheduled for 9 P.M. The hour came and went. Nothing happened. At 9:17 P.M., John Jewell heard groans from behind the curtain. The groans continued almost until 9:30 P.M. Jewell and Jeff Rosenzweig hoped the delay would last until midnight. If they did not execute Ricky Ray Rector by 12 A.M., Arkansas law required that a new death warrant must be issued. Perhaps Clinton would reconsider if the execution did not take place on schedule.

Behind the drawn curtain, technicians were search-

Ricky Ray Rector shortly before his execution

ing desperately for a vein in which to inject the poisons that would kill Rector. Eight times they tried and eight times they failed. Rector's veins kept collapsing. Shortly before 10 P.M., the technicians succeeded. The needle was in Ricky Ray Rector's vein. The execution would take place after all.

The curtain opened to reveal the last act of Ricky Ray Rector's unhappy life. The audience saw Rector enter, strapped to a gurney with a white bloodstained sheet covering him from his feet to his chin. The blood was Rector's, spilled during the technicians' search for a vein. Rector's beard was shaved. "He wants to look nice for his family," Jewell said.

Ricky Ray Rector's last words were: "Yes, I got baptized and saved." Rector said them in a flat voice as if they held little meaning for him.

Rector had a needle in his arm. It was connected to a tube that spiraled up into two bags of intravenous (IV) solution. The solution contained three chemicals that were sent slowly into his bloodstream. One was sodium pentothal, which causes unconsciousness by relaxing the muscles and depressing the central nervous system. The second was Pavulon, which blocks communication between nerves and muscles suppressing the respiratory system and helps stop the heart. The third was potassium chloride, which stops the heart altogether.

Jewell and Rosenzweig noticed that the fluids were slowly descending down the tubes and into Rector's body. "It looks like a hospital but instead of saving the patient, they're killing him," Jewell remarked. The chemicals spiraled down the tube into Rector's bloodstream, drop by deadly drop.

After a few moments, Rector said, "I'm getting dizzy." He gasped for air. His breathing became increasingly shallow. His lips stopped moving. His body shuddered. Then he died. In nineteen minutes, Rector's agony was over.

Ten months later, Bill Clinton was elected president of the United States. John Jewell speculated, "Perhaps if he had not been running for president, Clinton may

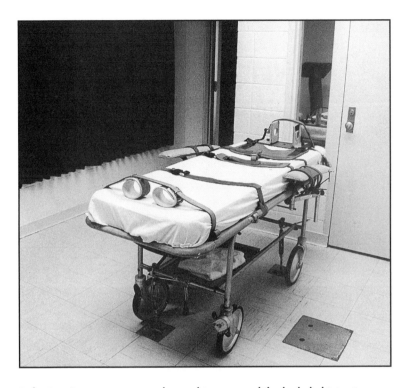

Ricky Ray Rector was strapped onto this gurney while the lethal injection was administered.

have commuted his sentence to life without parole. I'd like to think that anyhow."

John Jewell agreed with a fellow lawyer quoted in *The New Yorker*. He said that it was unfortunate for Rector that his case came up during a presidential campaign: "Poor ole Ricky Ray's timing just happened to be real bad."

SIX

 **An Appeal to the Supreme Court**

In the case described in this chapter, prisoner Dale Yates faced a death sentence. The only thing that stood between him and the electric chair was David Bruck, an attorney who specialized in the appeals process. Bruck's task was to convince the higher courts that Yates's legal rights had been violated at the trial level. Bruck ultimately took that argument all the way to the U.S. Supreme Court.

One evening in April 1981, Dale Yates and Henry Davis, two small-time criminals from semirural South Carolina, held up a small general store near the town of Tigerville. The robbery went haywire. When it was over, two people were dead. Henry Davis lay on the floor with six bullets in his body. Nearby was the body of Helen Wood, the sixty-three-year-old mother of the owner. Helen Wood lay with a knife wound in her heart. If the state of South Carolina had its way, Dale Yates would soon join them.

That Yates wound up on death row did not surprise most people who knew him. By the time he was ten years old, he and an older brother were sneaking into houses in the neighborhood when nobody was home to steal money. At fourteen, Yates was an accomplished car thief who stole cars to joyride. At sixteen, he

Dale Yates in elementary school

dropped out of school, hung around pool halls, smoked marijuana, stole more cars, and burglarized houses.

At seventeen, he and his brother were caught stealing, and setting fire to barns. Because of his previous record, Yates was sent to jail for nine years even though it was his first serious offense. After three years, he was paroled. It was a graduation of sorts. Jail had put the finishing touches on his criminal "education."

Yates managed to find a job in a plastic factory after he was released from prison. During the day, he made plastic pellets and molding. At night, he drank, got high on speed and marijuana, bought and sold drugs, and broke into homes and stores. "I don't know why really. Just for the hell of it," he said.

One day, he got into a fistfight at work and was fired. Shortly after that, according to Yates, he agreed to commit what he said was his first armed robbery. It was certainly his last. Yates planned the stick-up with his buddy Henry Davis and a friend of Davis's named David Loftos.

"I don't know who suggested it," Yates said. "We were sitting around one night, taking about how we needed money. We thought of a number of places we could rob but for some reason we dismissed them. I didn't like the idea. Maybe nobody did. I had done many burglaries but never an armed robbery. But once we started talking about it, we were in it."

The three men began to cruise around the area, looking for a good store to rob. Every place they passed seemed too risky. Then, Loftos left to meet his girlfriend at the mall. Yates and Davis continued to drive around looking for the right place. Finally, they selected a small general store in a little town called Tigerville. They parked and went inside.

The store was empty except for Willy Wood, the owner. The two men quickly approached the counter and Yates pulled out his gun. It was a .38 caliber. Davis had a knife, but he didn't show it at first. Yates did the talking. "Give me your money," he said. "What money?" Wood asked. "The money in your register," Yates responded.

Wood pressed down on the keys of the cash register and rang up "No Sale." He took $3,000 out of the drawer and handed it to Davis, who passed it to Yates. "Let's have the rest," said Yates. "There is no rest," Wood replied.

Davis drew his knife and told Wood to lean over the counter. Wood hesitated, realizing Davis meant to stab him. Davis shouted for Yates to shoot. Yates fired two bullets and fled, yelling to his partner as he ran, "Let's get out of here!"

Yates hopped into the car, started the motor, and waited for Davis. After what seemed like minutes but was probably seconds, he heard the sound of gunfire. Whatever was going on, Yates was not going to wait to find out. With a roar, he drove out of the parking space and headed down the highway, leaving his partner behind.

Luck was against Yates as he escaped. A doctor and his wife jogging along the road saw the car and later described it to the police. Yates drove onto a seldom-used dirt road off the highway. As he buried the money and the gun underneath some rocks, a tow truck passed by. The driver of the truck had heard the police report describing Yates's car over his CB radio and called in Yates's location.

Within minutes, the sheriff was pursuing Yates. Yates jumped out of his car and ran down a gully, desperately trying to escape. At the end of the gully, he looked up and found himself facing a policeman holding a gun aimed at his head.

When he was arrested, Yates learned what had happened after he had left the store. When he fired at Wood, the store owner threw up his hands to protect himself. One bullet hit his wrist. The other bullet missed. According to Wood's testimony at the trial, Davis had chased him around the store trying to stab him. As he did so, Wood's mother, Helen Wood, ran over from the post office next door to investigate the noise. As she stepped into the store, she ran right into Davis. He stabbed her once, the blade entering directly into her heart. Willy Wood meanwhile had managed to draw a gun and fired five bullets into Henry Davis, killing him.

Yates was arrested, taken to the police station, and charged with murder. Under the law in South Carolina and in most states, every participant in a felony crime is equally responsible for the death of an innocent victim, even if the participant did not carry out or even know about the killing: "The hand of one is the hand of all." Even though Yates did not know Helen Wood had been killed, or even intend her death, he was still charged with murder because he was an active participant in the robbery. For this, he could be sentenced to death.

Because the public defender who normally would have represented Yates was not available, the senior judge of the court asked a Greenville, South Carolina, attorney named John Mauldin to represent Yates.

Mauldin was an attorney with a good reputation specializing in criminal law. The judge asked him to be the lead lawyer.

"He pointed out to me that this was not just a simple murder case. The victim, Helen Wood, was a highly respected and well-liked member of the local Baptist community and her death devastated everyone. Her husband, Pralo Wood, was a retired member of the county sheriff's office. His brother was a retired state legislator. And Willy Wood's brother was the agent in charge of the Greenville Parole and Probation Board," Mauldin explained.

The judge told Mauldin that he was free to turn down the case. Mauldin thought about it and then agreed to take it.

I felt Dale [Yates] needed a good defense, and that if I refused, other lawyers would also refuse and Dale would not get the defense he deserved. Dale had several things in his favor. He didn't kill anybody. He wasn't the trigger man, and at that time, there was no one on South Carolina's death row who had not actually done the murder with which they had been charged. Also it seemed pretty clear that Henry [Davis] was the dominating figure in the robbery. If we could show how Dale was under Henry's influence, then we might save him from execution.

The prosecutor Mauldin faced was William W. Wilkins, a man Mauldin described as "the best trial lawyer I have ever come up against. He is absolutely extraordinary." Mauldin tried to make a deal for a plea bargain for his client. Often, in capital-punishment cases when the accused is not the trigger man, the state will allow the defendant to plead guilty to a lesser charge for which he will receive a life sentence.

Wilkins rejected the offer. "There was a lot of pressure for him to try the case in order to get the death penalty," Mauldin recalled.

When the trial started, John Mauldin felt the community's rage. "I received numerous death threats by telephone. The windshield of my car was smashed. I had to move out of my house during the trial to protect my family."

Although he was fearful, Mauldin did not back down. He continued to try to keep Yates from being executed. Mauldin tried to create doubt in the jury's mind concerning the murder charge. Since Yates had not killed anyone himself, Mauldin felt he had a chance. The big decision he had to make was whether or not to put Yates on the witness stand. Mauldin reasoned:

Letting a defendant testify can either make or break a case. Many times an attorney doesn't like to do so because once on the stand, his client may be asked all sorts of questions by the prosecutor that the defense would rather not introduce. Like his prior criminal record, for example. But since we had no other witness to what happened—Dale's partner was dead—the only way we could get certain information on the record—such as how [Henry] Davis dominated Dale [Yates], the heavy drinking that took place before the crime—was to have Dale supply it himself.

During the trial, Wilkins energetically attacked Yates's defense. He charged that Yates had intended to kill from the beginning because he fired the gun and had not bothered to cover his face during the robbery.

Yates did not help his cause when, on the witness stand, he said he felt remorse—for the death of his partner! Of the victim and her family, he said nothing.

"Sorry is a good word and juries like to hear that," Mauldin explained. "But you have to be sorry for the right thing. Yates was basically sorry for being caught and for his partner's death, and the jury picked up on that."

During the closing arguments, Wilkins released a bombshell. He suggested that Davis and Yates intended to kill Willy Wood in silence. He charged that they intended to stab him to death so that nobody would hear his murder take place. The argument made a powerful impression on the jury.

The defense tried to reinforce the fact that Yates had not harmed anyone and had been under the influence of Henry Davis. But there were too many obstacles to overcome. One problem was that the courts didn't use psychiatric evaluation at that time. The southern states were slow to introduce it in the courts, and poor defendants often paid the price. Mauldin explained:

It might have helped to have used psychiatric expert witnesses. At the time, they were just starting to be used [in South Carolina]. Today, I would have had Dale [Yates] given tests by professionals to show how he got to the point where he could have been involved in such a crime. The way he was raised by his parents, the influence of his older brother on his behavior. It would not have pardoned his crimes, but it would have helped explain them and perhaps made the jury more sympathetic.

So the jury found Yates guilty of murder. Then they deliberated over the penalty. The jury sent word to the judge: It was deadlocked over the death penalty. He ordered them to keep deliberating. Yates's hopes soared for a split decision. But it was not to happen. Shortly afterward, the jury returned and recommended unanimously that Yates be executed.

"I'll never forget the judge's words as long as I live," said Yates. " 'I sentence you to die on August 3, 1981. May God have mercy on your soul.' "

Yates expected to be executed in three months. He was not aware that it can take years to determine whether or not an execution sentence stands.

In every state of the Union, when a person is sentenced to death, an appeals process is automatically set in motion. At least one and often several courts review transcripts of the trial as well as any other information the defense lawyers can offer. These courts are called appeals courts, or appellate courts. They review only those cases that have been decided on the trial level.

In South Carolina, the appeal first goes back to the court in which the case was tried and, in death penalty cases, usually the federal courts. Many death penalty cases wind up at the highest court in the country—the Supreme Court of the United States. But in almost every appeal, the Supreme Court refuses to review the case. Then all that stands between the condemned person and death is the governor, who has the power to commute the death sentence to life in prison without parole.

The main issue that concerns the appeals courts is whether or not the defendant was given his full legal rights during the trial and the sentencing. If there was a serious error, the courts can order a new trial or, on occasion, the release of a defendant. This procedure is called "due process of law." The U.S. Constitution guarantees every individual due process of law. But in practice, many condemned people are denied full consideration of their rights, often on technical grounds. A lawyer's failure to file a legal document in a timely way, for example, can lead to his client being executed—even if there is evidence that the client is innocent.

When a case is reviewed, the appeals courts examine the record to see if errors took place during the trial. Was there racial discrimination during selection of the jury? Did the judge give the jury wrong instructions? Was testimony allowed that should not have been? Was evidence introduced that should not have been? Did the prosecutor withhold evidence that would have been helpful to the defendant? Did the defense attorney properly represent the defendant? Did the judge allow inflammatory remarks to be made? Is there new evidence that should be considered?

Dale Yates knew his case was particularly difficult because he had admitted to robbing the store and shooting at the owner. His defense was that because he did not kill Helen Wood, his death sentence should be commuted to a life sentence. His only hope was that the courts would reverse his sentence and allow him to be retried on that issue alone. The main question now was: Was there a significant error during the trial that could convince the appeals court that Yates should have a new trial or, at least, a new sentencing trial? How this question was answered was literally the difference between life and death for Yates.

Yates's case went through two appeals in the South Carolina courts and was turned down. It was at this point that the case came to the attention of David Bruck, who was working in the state's public defender's office. His specialty was capital-punishment cases. "These are the hardest cases to try because they involve men and women who have been convicted of killing someone—and now you are asking the state or the federal courts to reverse a sentence already imposed by a judge and jury," he says.

For David Bruck, his work is an expression of his principles. He is completely opposed to the death penalty. He says:

The death penalty is wrong because it is irrevocable, because it does not deter, and because it cannot be applied fairly. Society reserves the death penalty for the poorest, the weakest, and often the ugliest members of its society. I am not a bleeding heart. Some of the crimes that my clients have committed are repulsive and my heart goes out to the victims and their survivors. But this in no way justifies another death, no matter how horrible the crime.

David Bruck is considered one of the best appeals lawyers in the United States in death penalty cases. Out of more than fifty clients, only three have been executed. Bruck considers himself lucky: "Sometimes, to save people, you have to work miracles. You often grab at straws and find that the straw holds." Bruck's job was to review entire trial records, talk to his clients, reexamine the evidence presented, meet with the original trial's lawyers, and identify where errors may have been made.

Although Bruck is a Canadian, he sometimes gives the impression of being a Southerner. His manner is gentlemanly, even courtly at times. In his mid-forties, the prematurely graying Bruck is self-contained, deliberate in his thoughts and movement, and extremely knowledgeable. In South Carolina, a state in which an overwhelming majority favors the death penalty, Bruck has gained the respect of many who oppose him.

In a *New York Times* article (July 21, 1995), Dick Hartpoolian, a former prosecutor who had argued against Bruck on several appeals recalled, "I worked with some of the foremost prosecution experts in the country to get ready for that argument and they didn't know one-tenth of 1 percent of what he knew." One case, Hartpoolian recalled, involved a man who murdered a woman during a robbery:

David noticed that the jury, before recommending sentence, had not been told that if the defendant was sentenced to prison, he would never be eligible for parole. Bruck knew this was a hot issue in many states and that the Supreme Court would soon be called on to deal with it. Bruck raised the issue and the Supreme Court ordered the case retried. He has that dimension of not only trying a case but of anticipating what the law may be in the future.

Bruck lives in Columbia, South Carolina, where he has practiced law for almost twenty-five years. He handles only one kind of case—men and women on death row. While most of his cases begin after someone has already been sentenced to death, Bruck has, on occasion, handled cases on the trial level.

In 1995, David Bruck represented Susan Smith, who made national headlines after she confessed to murdering her two sons, aged fourteen months and two years. She strapped them into their car seats and pushed her car into a lake, drowning them. The prosecutor had sought the death penalty on the grounds that the murder was planned in advance. Bruck successfully argued that she had killed her children on the spur of the moment. She was sentenced to life in prison without parole.

Bruck came to Columbia, South Carolina, during the height of the Vietnam War. Strongly opposed to America's involvement in Vietnam, he became active in the antiwar movement while attending law school at the University of South Carolina. He helped provide legal counseling for U.S. soldiers stationed in the area. He also helped publish an underground, antiwar newspaper that was distributed to the U.S. soldiers.

After the war, David Bruck was prepared to return to Canada when he became involved in a trial in which some of his friends were being harassed for their antiwar activities. One day, while he was in the court, he observed a capital-punishment case in which two brothers were on trial for robbing and killing a store owner. The incompetence of the defense lawyer angered him. It is still, unfortunately, a common problem for poor defendants. Bruck says:

Many poor people feel that they will stand a better chance in court if they have a lawyer they can pay for rather than a public defender. The family doesn't have much money, so often the lawyer they hire isn't very good. As a result, they don't defend their client properly and he winds up either getting a long sentence or being sentenced to death. If they had a good attorney, he might have won his client a lighter sentence—or even acquittal.

So Bruck approached the public defender's office and offered them a deal. He would represent all their capital-punishment cases on a part-time basis for a salary of $10,000 a year. "I felt privileged to do something that was important for me to do rather than work just to make money," he said. By the time Dale Yates's case reached his desk in 1981, Bruck's job was full-time and his salary somewhat higher.

When Bruck reviewed Dale Yates's case, it seemed cut and dried. Yates had admitted to carrying out the

Attorney David Bruck meets with his client, Dale Yates, in prison to discuss the appeal of Yates's death sentence.

robbery. He had a gun and he shot the store owner, wounding him, while his partner later killed a woman. There seemed little Bruck could do to convince the South Carolina Supreme Court that they should order a new trial concerning the sentencing part of the case. Late one night, as he was preparing his argument to the South Carolina Supreme Court, Bruck once again reviewed the testimony. Something bothered him. He felt that a mistake had been made, but where? Although the case against Yates seemed airtight, his instincts told him that there was an error somewhere.

It was close to midnight when he found it. The judge had instructed the jury before it began deliberating that they could presume malice on Yates's part because he was armed—that is, because Yates carried a gun. And if there was malice, it made no difference whether or not Yates had carried out the killing. As long as Yates intended to kill, and somebody was killed during the crime in which he took part, then Yates was equally responsible for the death.

Bruck recognized that the trial judge had made a serious error by telling the jury that, without proof, they could assume Yates intended to kill. The Supreme Court had recently ruled that it was the jury, not the judge, who had to determine malice. Malice could not be presumed. If the jury decided that Yates had intended to kill somebody, he could be executed. But the jury, not the judge, had to make that determination.

Bruck presented this argument to the South Carolina Supreme Court. The court was not impressed. They unanimously rejected the appeal—five to zero—without providing any explanation. Bruck was not surprised. He appealed the case directly to the Supreme Court. Although the Supreme Court usually turns down most requests to review death penalty cases, Bruck was hopeful.

"I felt that we had a chance that the Supreme Court would at least look at this case because it involved a recent decision they had made," he said. "The Supreme Court expects the state courts to abide by its rulings and it doesn't like its decisions to be ignored."

Bruck's instinct was correct. The Supreme Court suggested that the South Carolina court reconsider this case in light of its most recent decision. The South Carolina court responded, perhaps somewhat arrogantly, that the recent Supreme Court decision did not apply to the case. But the decision now was four to one.

"South Carolina was telling the Supreme Court, in effect, thank you very much but we know how to handle our affairs down here and we don't need any help from you. That doesn't sit well with the Supreme Court," Bruck explained.

Bruck appealed the case once again to the Supreme Court. This time the Supreme Court gave the case a full review. It reprimanded the South Carolina court, saying in no uncertain terms that their earlier ruling did indeed apply to this case and that they needed to look at it again.

The South Carolina court continued to resist. It stated that while the Supreme Court decision was applicable in the Yates case, the error was "harmless" and did not affect the case's outcome. However, the vote was now three to two in favor of denying Yates's request for a new sentencing trial. The judges were beginning to get the message.

Once again, David Bruck returned to the Supreme Court and once again the Supreme Court unanimously came down on South Carolina. They made it clear that the error was not "harmless." By this time, Bruck felt that victory was near. He explained: "What the Supreme Court was telling South Carolina, in essence, [was] that unless you can show strong support for this error to be 'harmless,' you should order a new sentencing trial. We are not going to allow you to execute this man unless you do."

Shortly after the decision, Bruck got a call from the prosecutor's office. After a few moments of polite conversation, the prosecutor came to the point. The state did not want to retry the case and was willing to make a deal. If Yates would accept life imprisonment—which meant a minimum of twenty years before he would be eligible for parole—the state would not retry him.

When Bruck told Yates about the offer, he joyfully accepted. "When I got the news, everyone in the prison knew it. They could hear me yellin' and whooping," he later said.

Today, Dale Yates is forty years old. He is incarcerated in Leesville Correctional Center in Bishopville, South Carolina. He has become a model prisoner and a born-again Christian. "Jesus has become the center of my life," he says. He says he is determined to lead a righteous life.

Yates goes to the parole board for the first time in the year 2001. One man who will oppose his parole is Willy Wood. He will never forget the bullet that Dale Yates fired at him or the body of his mother, lying lifeless on the floor with a knife in her heart. As far as he is concerned, Dale Yates should have been executed. He has been quoted as saying, "I'd pull the switch right now, free of charge."

Yates was lucky. His case came at a time when the courts had more concern for the rights of the condemned. Since then, the federal and state courts have increasingly narrowed and restricted the rights of the condemned to appeal their sentences. Time limits have been set on the introduction of new evidence and the periods within which defense lawyers can file appeals. Bruck notes:

People often think that murderers get off on technicalities when what really happens is that people are more likely to be executed on technicalities. In one Georgia case, two people were convicted of murder, a woman and a man she hired to murder her husband. Both were sentenced to death. The woman's lawyer appealed the sentence on the grounds that an error had been made and got her sentence changed to life. The lawyer for the man failed to make the same appeal in time and the courts told him, "Sorry, you were too late in filing your appeal." The man was executed.

Today, John Mauldin no longer asks juries to consider mercy. "It's a waste of time to ask for mercy," he says. "Juries today don't want to hear about mercy. They may listen to unusual circumstances, but not pleas for mercy, especially if someone was killed while another crime was being committed."

David Bruck points out that, in the end, the identity of the individual who actually gets executed is a matter of indifference to the state:

David Bruck (left) and prosecutor Dick Hartpoolian outside the U.S. Supreme Court

The system is so unjust. It's like a lottery. Names are put in and dragged out. The state treats people very blindly. I don't justify or excuse their crimes, nor do I ask the courts to. What I ask is that people be allowed to live. Those who I represent have had such horribly hard lives that it's hard to understand why they receive so little pity. There's no question in my mind that the death sentence is intended solely for the poor and racial minorities. They are people who, when society looks at them, feel that there is not going to be any loss at their death.

Perhaps death penalty cases illustrate most strongly the importance of defense lawyers. Without competent attorneys to defend the accused, the American criminal justice system has no chance of working—and innocent people will pay for that failure with their lives.

 # Glossary

acquitted—discharged completely from an accusation

appeal—a legal proceeding by which a case is brought from a lower court for a rehearing. The appeals court rules on whether the legal rights of the person appealing have been denied, rather than on matters of fact.

appellate courts—courts that hear an appeal on the state or federal level. They have the power to review, reverse, modify, or affirm judgments made by lower courts. Federal courts have power over state courts. The most powerful appellate court is the U.S. Supreme Court, which deals with issues of constitutional rights.

attorney general—the chief law officer for a state or the federal government

bench warrant—a document issued by a judge or a court allowing a police officer to arrest a person who has violated a court order

charge—an accusation brought against a person for violating the law

charge the jury—to give the jury instructions on points of law that must govern their actions as they deliberate

closing argument—the final statement to a jury given by the prosecutor and defense attorney before the jury deliberates on the verdict

commutation—a reduction of a sentence, such as commuting a death sentence to life in prison without parole

criminal court—the court in which defendants are tried for breaking the law

criminal defense lawyers—attorneys who specialize in cases involving criminal law

criminal justice system—all the governmental institutions involved in enforcing criminal law, including the police, courts, prosecutors, and defense lawyers

criminal law or code—the branch of law that involves crimes

cross-examine—to question a witness by challenging the accuracy of his or her previous testimony

defendant—a person accused of breaking the law or required to answer in a civil case

district attorney—a prosecuting officer who represents the state or federal government in trials and hearings

family or **juvenile court**—a court that handles family disputes between husbands and wives, and cases concerning the welfare, support, and custody of children. This kind of court also handles cases involving young people, usually under the age of sixteen, who have committed serious crimes.

felony—a serious crime, such as murder, rape, robbery, arson, or drug dealing, as defined by law

grand jury—a group of people, or jury, responsible for examining accusations of crime to determine if there is enough evidence to charge a defendant

homicide—a criminal act involving the taking of a human life

hostile witness—a witness whose prejudiced opinions are revealed during questioning by the defense or prosecution in a trial

indict—to charge a person with a crime

jury—a group of men and women, usually twelve people, who are required to deliver a verdict in a case according to the evidence presented

juvenile delinquent—someone, usually sixteen years old or younger, who has committed an act that would be considered a crime if it were committed by an adult

larceny—the unlawful taking of property by theft, embezzlement, fraud, or trick without the other person's consent

objection—the act of objecting during a trial to a statement made by a witness, a question asked by the opposing attorney, or the introduction of evidence not allowed by the rules of the court. If the judge sustains the objection, the jury cannot consider the testimony or the question must be withdrawn.

opening argument—the introductory statement to the jury made by the prosecution and the defense outlining what they will prove or disprove during the trial

overrule—to deny an attorney's objection to a question or a statement made by the opposing side

pardon—an official statement ending the penalty imposed upon someone for a crime

plea bargain—an agreement between a defendant, the prosecution, and the judge in which the defendant agrees to plead guilty to a lesser charge

pro bono—taking on legal work without pay as a public service; a Latin term meaning "for the good"

prosecutor—a person who conducts proceedings for the state against the defendant in a criminal case

public defender—a lawyer who represents accused persons who cannot afford to pay for legal service in criminal matters

robbery—the taking of property by force (or the threat of force) from another person without consent

 # A Note on Sources

The author drew on trial transcripts and original inter-
views for the information about the cases in this book.
He referred to articles from several newspapers and
magazines, including *The New Yorker*, *Newsweek*, and the
New York Times, and the following books: Johnnie L.
Cochran, *Journey to Justice* (New York: Ballantine Books,
1996); James Kunen, *How Can You Defend Those People:
The Making of a Criminal Lawyer* (New York: Random
House, 1983); Peter Neufeld, Barry Scheck, and James
Dwyer, *Actual Innocence* (New York: Doubleday, 2000);
and Lawrence Schiller and James Willwerth, *An
American Tragedy, The Uncensored Story of the Simpson
Defense* (New York: Random House, 1996).

 # For Further Information

Books

Aaseng, Nathan. *The O.J. Simpson Trial: What It Shows Us about Our Legal System.* New York: Walker & Company, 1996.

Farish, Leah. *The First Amendment: Freedom of Speech, Religion, and the Press.* Springfield, NJ: Enslow Publishers, 1998.

Gottfried, Ted. *Capital Punishment: The Death Penalty Debate.* Springfield, NJ: Enslow Publishers, 1997.

Henson, Judge Burt, and Ross R. Olney. *Furman v. Georgia: The Constitution and the Death Penalty.* New York: Franklin Watts, 1996.

Jacobs, Thomas A., et al. *What Are My Rights?: 95 Questions and Answers about Teens and the Law.* Minneapolis, MN: Free Spirit Publishing, 1997.

Pascoe, Elaine. *America's Courts on Trial: Questioning Our Legal System.* Brookfield, CT: Millbrook Press, 1997.

Patrick, John J. *The Young Oxford Companion to the Supreme Court of the United States.* New York: Oxford University Press Children's Books, 1994.

Sheindlin, Judy, and Josh Getlin (contributor). *Don't Pee on My Leg and Tell Me It's Raining: America's Toughest Family Court Judge Speaks Out.* New York: HarperCollins, 1997.

Silverstein, Herma. *Threads of Evidence: Using Forensic Science to Solve Crimes.* New York: Twenty-First Century Books, 1996.

Wice, Paul B. *Gideon v. Wainwright and the Right to Counsel.* New York: Franklin Watts, 1995.

Zeinert, Karen. *Free Speech: From Newspapers to Music Lyrics.* Springfield, NJ: Enslow Publishers, 1995.

Organizations

For further information about criminal justice in the United States and careers in the legal profession, contact the following organizations.

American Bar Association
Service Center
541 North Fairbanks Court
Chicago, IL 60611
312/988-5522
http://www.abanet.org/

Innocence Project at Cardozo Law School
55 Fifth Avenue
New York, NY 10003
212/790-0354
http://www.criminaljustice.org/PUBLIC/cardozo.htm

The Legal Aid Society of New York
36 West 44th Street
New York, NY 10036
212/840-6377
http://www.legal-aid.org/

National Association of Criminal Defense Lawyers (NACDL)
1025 Connecticut Avenue, N.W.
Suite 901
Washington, DC 20036
202/872-8600
http://www.criminaljustice.org

Neighborhood Defender Service of Harlem
2031 Fifth Avenue
2nd Floor
New York, New York 10035
212/876-5500
http://www.ndsny.org/

Supreme Court of the United States
Public Information Office
Washington, DC 20543
202/479-3211
http://www.supremecourtus.gov/index.html

Index

Numbers in *italics* indicate illustrations

 # About the Author

Richard Wormser is an accomplished documentary filmmaker and writer who has produced, written, or directed more than 100 films. He is the author of fifteen young adult titles for various publishers, including *The Rise and Fall of Jim Crow: The African-American Struggle against Discrimination: 1865–1954,* available from Franklin Watts. Richard Wormser lives in New York City.